No One Has
to Die Alone

No One Has to Die Alone

Preparing for a Meaningful Death

Lani Leary, PhD

Foreword by Jean Watson

ATRIA PAPERBACK
New York London Toronto Sydney New Delhi

BEYOND WORDS
Hillsboro, Oregon

ATRIA PAPERBACK
A Division of Simon & Schuster, Inc.
1230 Avenue of the Americas
New York, NY 10020

BEYOND WORDS
20827 N.W. Cornell Road, Suite 500
Hillsboro, Oregon 97124-9808
503-531-8700 / 503-531-8773 fax
www.beyondword.com

Managing editor: Lindsay S. Brown
Developmental editor: Emily Han
Copyeditor: Ali McCart
Proofreader: Linda Meyer
Design: Devon Smith
Composition: William H. Brunson Typography Services

First Atria Paperback/Beyond Words trade paperback edition April 2012

ATRIA PAPERBACK and colophon are trademarks of Simon & Schuster, Inc.
Beyond Words Publishing is a division of Simon & Schuster, Inc.

For more information about special discounts for bulk purchases,
please contact Simon & Schuster Special Sales at 1-866-506-1949 or
business@simonandschuster.com.

The Simon & Schuster Speakers Bureau can bring authors to your live event.
For more information or to book an event, contact the Simon & Schuster Speakers
Bureau at 1-866-248-3049 or visit our website at www.simonspeakers.com.

Manufactured in the United States of America

10 9 8 7 6 5 4 3 2 1

Library of Congress Cataloging-in-Publication Data
    Leary, Lani.
        No one has to die alone : preparing for a meaningful death / by Lani Leary. —
    1st paperback ed.
            p.   cm.
    1. Death.   2. Caregiving.   3. Grief.   4. Grief in children.   I. Title.
    HQ1073.L425   2012
    306.9—dc23
                                                                      2011042995

ISBN: 978-1-58270-352-7
ISBN: 978-1-4516-6500-0 (eBook)

The corporate mission of Beyond Words Publishing, Inc.: *Inspire to Integrity*

Dedicated to the memory of
Marjorie Chivers Leary (1921–1967)
and Robert Thomas Leary (1919–2003)

CONTENTS

FOREWORD

This is a book of grace, beauty, blessings, and guidance for anyone wishing to expand their consciousness and their practical, as well as sacred, relationship with death, dying, and human suffering—the fear, pain, joy, privilege, struggle, and success on this path.

As someone with a background in nursing and as an author of the theories, ethics, and philosophies of human caring (caring science as a humanistic expanded model of science), I have a deep understanding of working with nurses and health professionals around the world. Because of my commitment to improving human caring, I created Watson Caring Science Institute (www.watsoncaringscience.org).

No One Has to Die Alone is a philosophy; an ethic; a moral, humane, and concrete map into this territory—this unknown mystery and miracle we all face. This beautiful work is an experiential and spiritual guide as well as an inspiring workbook for the public, for caregivers, for all health and healing professionals, and for lay citizens, children and adults alike. It is a reminder that we all have much to learn and to live through with our own dying preparation, the dying experiences of our loved ones, and our mourning.

This book shares stories and practical applications for those who wish to support loved ones but feel stymied or scared about how to do so. When most lack the experience and thus the confidence to help, Lani Leary shows us the possibility and power of our participation ... and then she shows us how to do it. Her stories demonstrate that making a difference is possible; her examples cross cultural, gender, and age differences to invite us all into our last opportunity to show love. Lani gives us shining stories of how everyday men, women, and children can advocate for support, and respond to their loved ones. She weaves together personal and universal considerations as well as practical and emotional aspects of facing, responding to, and being with death and grief. Lani offers simple solutions that can be used in overwhelming emotional, spiritual, and physical challenges. This book leaves us with the hope that we can do more than just manage death but can also heal and grow in the process.

This is not just a book for professionals but is also a valuable resource for family and friends of caregivers and those looking to prepare for the inevitable future when someone they love faces death. It is also a book for *you*. It can help you reflect upon how you would like to die and what you will value at the end of your life. It can help you and your family prepare for a meaningful and authentic death while guiding you to help others.

No One Has to Die Alone challenges our commonly held myths about death and asks us to reconsider our fears and assumptions. It is a book that enlarges possibilities and perspectives. Lani presents us with questions such as: How might we respond differently if we knew that we could make a difference? How might our grief be different if we knew that death could not sever a relationship? This book invites us to ask more questions, to feel comfortable with silence, and to practice a sacred presence with a loved one. We begin to consider that we do not have to be afraid of impending death and that there is another way to be present with *what is* rather than to deny or ignore the opportunities we are given. Lani challenges us to consider the dying journey as a gift, a chance to give and receive the love that is most essential to all of us.

Lani's experience as a bereaved teenager can speak to the young reader who wants to help but doesn't know how. It will broaden the circle of care so that adult caregivers include the younger generation as integral members of a caring team. Her story of how her near-death experience informed her work and changed her ability to comfort the dying and the bereaved will diminish your fear of death and give you hope. She shares the lessons she was taught during her extensive work with dying patients. Her suggestions for activities, conversations, and ways of being with your dying loved one will leave you empowered. Lani describes the healing that happens for both the dying and the bereaved when we participate and offer ourselves to the challenge. This book delivers and, as Lani writes, leaves us believing we can "feel gratitude rather than grief, and love rather than loss."

In essence, this book inspires new visions in society and conversations between families and loved ones, inviting us to come closer to death as a living, healing return to the mystery. It gives us courage to embrace the profound needs of the living and the dying as we cocreate, shape, and participate in the sacred circle of life and death.

Jean Watson, PhD, RN, AHN-BC, FAAN, is a distinguished professor of nursing at the University of Colorado College of Nursing and holds the Murchinson-Scoville Endowed Chair in Caring Science at Anschutz Medical Center Campus, Colorado. Jean is also the founder of Watson Caring Science Institute, a nonprofit foundation to expand and authentically sustain human caring and healing for individuals and all of humanity.

PREFACE

How we die matters. Most dying patients report that they fear the isolation and loneliness of dying more than the pain or the finality of death. Loved ones want to be of service but are paralyzed from fear, lack of skills, and an absence of exposure to the most universal life experience. We can learn how to play a significant role in helping the dying, their family, and the community face the transition of death. We can learn new attitudes, perspectives, and skills that will help us help others and even ourselves.

Modern healthcare has changed not only the way we live but also the way we respond to our most vulnerable members of society during illness and aging. Until two generations ago, people usually died suddenly, after an accident or a serious illness. Currently, most of us expect our dying to take longer, which necessitates more decision making, caregiving, and resources. This practical book offers lessons in the form of supportive references, useful tools, vocabulary, questions, real-life letters and stories, and appendixes with further resources, so readers can pick up the book at any point and apply the information to their personal challenge.

This book is a road map through illness, death, and bereavement. It outlines how to begin the process of support, how to stay the course, and how to walk away with a sense of peace and gratitude. It shows you how to make a difference in the life and death of your loved one. I share the stories and lessons with you because so many people have asked me how I did it. I've been asked how I was able to watch the pain, get through my fears, know what to do, and intuit how to help. I pass on the legacy of skills and attitudes that I learned in my work at the bedside of more than five hundred patients as they died. I listened and observed how I might be of service so that they could be at peace physically, emotionally, and spiritually as they coped with illness and let go into death. My work as a psychotherapist, hospice counselor, professional listener, and lay chaplain in the intensive care unit of a hospital and in the homes of private clients across the country has given me the expertise and confidence to respond to others' unique needs. My near-death experience and the insight I gained provided me with a strong visceral conviction and with the spiritual assurance that we are more than merely a physical body—our consciousness lives on, and love trumps death.

Others have asked what it would take for them to be able to do the same for their loved one. My background as an educator and a researcher allows me the opportunity to teach what I have learned experientially and didactically so that others can put the skills, attitudes, and knowledge into action. I have heard back from many family members, clients, and students that a skill or perspective they learned from me gave them the needed direction and confidence to be of service, and that their intervention made a difference to the dying person, themselves, and their family. This book is the collection of my twenty-eight years of education, research, and experience put forth so you can bring this knowledge home and begin making your own personal difference in your loved one's dying journey. My greatest hope is that you will use this book and be able to be of service to your loved ones, and that in the end, you will know they have not died alone.

I believe our best life is made up of small kindnesses and that to serve one person is to serve the world; to be of service to those in need is different than helping them. Rachel Naomi Remen, MD, described the distinction well when she wrote that helping is a form of inequality and may take more away from people than it could ever give them. When we learn to serve, we bring our whole selves, our limitations, our wounds, and even our challenges. Remen believes that service is a relationship between equals that contributes to wholeness, rather than to the brokenness in others and in ourselves. Though you may not believe that you have the courage or the know-how to be of service in the world of the dying, you make great progress by taking small steps and building your competency one lesson at a time.[1] One such step is picking up this book.

Perhaps you are picking up this book in an airport as you travel from one coast to another in hopes of seeing your father before he dies. Maybe you have just received a phone call from your best friend telling you that she is awaiting the report from a breast biopsy, and you want to be prepared to respond in a helpful way. Or you want to be able to make healthcare decisions for yourself to relieve your loved ones of having to guess about your wishes. Or you want to help your children to not be fearful as they encounter the natural cycles of life. This book can help you.

We can be caught off guard and feel ill prepared, ambushed, and sideswiped by a life-threatening diagnosis. When it counts most, we can be paralyzed with self-doubt, and fear might make us unable to respond to our loved one's needs. Or after responding, we waste our waning energy by second-guessing our decisions and feeling guilty. Most of us only learn about death and grief in a crash course. There is another way to navigate this challenging time, and we can gather resources ahead of time. We can prepare by understanding the dying and grieving processes, and the dying person's accompanying needs. We can rehearse and find less demanding opportunities to strengthen our confidence and competency. Experiences can be shored up so that when the time comes, suddenly or gradually, we know we can cope. We can earn the confidence to make a difference, and we will move toward our loved one rather than away from the last opportunity to demonstrate love.

We can learn skills to be of service to our loved ones so they can die well, meaning that people facing death have more choice, more comfort, more companionship, and more authenticity. Together, we can change the culture, myths, and taboos associated with death and dying and replace them with new attitudes, competencies, and ways of being with the dying. We can improve the unacceptable loneliness and isolation that others experience as they die. Through compassion and facing our fears, we can change the ways we prepare and accept our own inevitable death. National Vital Statistics Reports indicate that roughly 10 percent of the population dies suddenly and unexpectedly; 90 percent of us will die from an illness of some length.[2] The importance of knowing this trend is that we can prepare *now* to live fully, even in the face of death, once we have confronted our fears, assumptions, and myths about death and dying. We have time *now* to decide who we want to care for us, what life-sustaining measures we want in certain circumstances, where we want to die and with whom. We can write our living wills and designate a healthcare power of attorney before we need them; we can organize our affairs as a gift of simplicity for our survivors; we can make our own funeral arrangements and write our own obituaries; we can begin to say those things that are the most important. We can live authentically right up to the moment of our death.

Assumptions, Beliefs, and Experiences

- I believe that how we die matters to the people who are shedding this life and to their loved ones. To die with

our choices and values means that we live right up to
the moment of our death. Abdicating choices about
how we die leaves a different legacy. And I believe these
choices affect how survivors grieve. Death prepares
future generations for a life lived with awareness, compassion, and appreciation rather than denial, avoidance,
and fear.

- I believe that how we die has more to do with our
  choices than with the physiology of illness. We can all
  make better choices that positively affect the quality of
  how we die. Evidence shows that when patients are
  given information and choice, they will make decisions
  for palliative comfort care and hospice care over
  aggressive hospital interventions and, as a result, will
  have a better quality of life and will often live longer.
  The emotional and financial costs to patients and families are significantly reduced.

- I believe we can learn to be present and compassionate
  throughout the illness and death of our loved ones. We
  can learn to make informed choices and practice new
  skills in order to help our loved ones die more peacefully and authentically. We can make a difference.

- I believe that enhancing the quality of a person's
  death enhances the quality of our life. I believe that
  those who engage and participate in the death of their
  loved ones experience their grief in a softer way than
  those who, for whatever reason, do not participate.
  Participation and service heal us all at the deepest
  emotional level.

- I believe that your personal presence is the strongest
  antidote to a dying person's greatest pain, which is their
  loneliness.

NOTES

1. Rachel Naomi Remen, MD, interview by Dr. Jeffrey Mishlove, *Thinking Allowed: Conversations on the Leading Edge of Knowledge and Discovery*, http://www.william james.com/transcripts/remen.htm.

2. Centers for Disease Control and Prevention, *National Vital Statistics Reports* 59, no. 4 (March 16, 2011), http://www.cdc.gov/nchs/data/nvsr/nvsr59/nvsr59_04.pdf.

Betsy Murphy, FNP, CHPN, "It's About Life," *Today's Caregiver* (April 16, 2008), http://www.caregiver.com/articles/general/its_about_life.htm.

ACKNOWLEDGMENTS

As many authors before me have confessed, this book would never have been written without the inspiration and support of many people I've known throughout my life.

I hope to share what I learned while at the bedside of hundreds of people who were dying. My profound gratitude goes to those patients and their families who included me in a sacred space and time surrounding their deaths, and in doing so gave me invaluable opportunities to companion, share, and grow. They taught me far more than I ever gave them. It is my hope that what they taught me can become my gift to you. The time I spent with them showed me that people can die with peace and without fear, rather than in isolation and desperation. This book is intended to make a difference: for you, for your loved ones, for future generations and caregivers.

So I gratefully acknowledge the hospice patients, from Eva through Jack, who enriched my life, and their family members who shared their feelings of gratitude rather than regret.

I also am deeply grateful to students I have worked with over the years for their questions, fears, and reactions so I could teach others how to intervene and respond with compassion and skill. I owe a debt of gratitude to my clients as well, who came to me for therapy to treat such issues as depression, addiction, and anxiety often to find that these were symptoms of loss and grief. I am humbled by their trust.

My sincere thanks go to the selfless mavericks of thanatology—death and dying—who brought death out into the open and added compassionate understanding to our lives. I am particularly grateful to Elisabeth Kübler-Ross, Dame Cicely Saunders, Alan Wolfelt, Stephen and Ondrea Levine, Helen Fitzgerald, Therese Rando, Ken Doka, and scholars in the Association for Death Education and Counseling.

I am humbled by the validation and support given by the Seattle chapter of the International Association for Near-Death Studies, especially from Kim Clark Sharp, Greg Wilson, and Ken Ring.

Then there are the angels in my life who, in various ways, encouraged, prodded, and kept me on track so this book would see completion. My heartfelt thanks to all who read multiple drafts and offered feedback: Cynthia Smith, Judy McConnell, Sioux Plummer Douglas, Laurie Hessel, Roger and Peggy Ponto, Sally Murphy, Nancy Collins, Marilyn Cade, and Clarke Van Sice.

Grateful words will never be enough for those who are closest to me. I'm thankful every day for the comfort, healing, and love that were shown me during and after my father's death. I am especially grateful for my husband, Rick Houck, for his daily support, and for my lifelong friend Paul Silen, who traveled halfway around the world to validate my feelings. To my daughter, Whitney Houck: you are my greatest teacher. I love you and thank you for surprising me daily by demonstrating how much we can make a difference when we just pay attention from the heart.

This book would not have been launched without the generosity of spirit that my childhood friend and author Dale Hope extended to me, and the encouragement and guidance provided by agent extraordinaire Chuck Morrell. Chuck's clarity and confidence led me into the skillful hands of publisher Cynthia Black, editors Emily Han and Lindsay

Brown, and other publishing midwives at Beyond Words Publishing and Simon & Schuster. They have all become family to me, and the process of birthing this book has been a joy and a labor of love.

Mahalo nui loa,
Lani Leary, PhD
Kaneohe, Hawaii 2011

How to Use This Book

This book is divided into two halves of the journey through dying and grieving. Chapters one through five—the five things I wish I had known about death—address perspectives to help a loved one or caregiver through the process of dying. In the second half, I present the five things I wish I had known about grief to help survivors grieve in preparation for and after the death of their loved one. I have organized the chapters so they can be read in any order, and information is not dependent on previous chapters. I have tried to provide a set of vocabulary, skills, and examples so the concepts are practical and immediately applicable.

I start with my own personal journey in hopes that you might identify and know that you are not alone. People have told me it is beneficial to have metaphors, examples, role models, and stories with which to relate. Many feel relieved to be given the words to help express this new landscape in which they find themselves.

I offer dialogues as a way to begin conversations with loved ones because, after all, you may have never had to discuss a fatal diagnosis or a terminal prognosis before and may not know where to begin. You can personalize these examples and apply them to your situation. I conclude with a comprehensive appendix of resources, organizations, books, and links that you may find helpful to explore options, research information, or be in touch with others in similar situations.

Thank you for your interest in being of service, and for the difference you will make in the life and death of another human being.

Part I

Making a Difference through Illness, Dying, and Death

INTRODUCTION

MY STORY

I have come full circle. Unable to help my mother during her death when I was thirteen years old, I was left with grief exacerbated by regret and guilt. In order to cope and make my way up into life again, I vowed that I would never again regret not knowing how to make a difference or not taking action. This is the story of how I made my way out of the clutches of unresolved grief and into a peace that allowed me to usher my father peacefully out of his life thirty-six years later, grieving but grateful.

I walk into our kitchen. My mother is standing at the kitchen sink, whistling to the red cardinals in the plumeria tree. As I hurry to slip past her, she turns and looks at me as though her gaze could wrap its arms around me. "I love you so much," she says softly. I roll my eyes and tsk, responding as an independent thirteen-year-old striking out to sever the umbilical cord. My mother is cut down to silence.

Without warning, a week later my eight-year-old brother wakes me in the morning saying, "Mommy's sick, and she's throwing up." I respond as I think she would and bring her a tray with cinnamon-sugar toast and orange juice. I tell her I will take my brothers down to the playground so she can sleep. When we return three hours later, her bed is empty. There is a note from a neighbor saying that she has taken my mother to the hospital. A neighbor comes over to stay with us while our father is with our mother in the hospital long into the night. It is a long, lonely day and night without answers. I write a letter to God trying to describe my confusion and asking God to let her come home.

The next day my grandparents fly in from California to visit their daughter and grandchildren. It feels like a vacuum in the house: the air is still, people move slowly, and no one speaks about what is happening. I am too afraid to ask questions. My father and grandparents go to the hospital and tell us it is better that we wait at home. That evening my grandmother bursts into the living room, hysterical, and I cannot understand what she is saying. My grandfather follows her into the house, comes to me, and holds me. "Your mother took a turn for the worse," he says gently. *At least she's not dead*, I say silently to myself. And then he follows with, "She died tonight."

My parents had not talked to my two younger brothers and me about the Guillain-Barre syndrome that had already cut short the lives of six out of eight patients diagnosed in our state. We did not understand what the illness was or that it could cause my mother's death. We did not know about the unpredictable and intractable pain associated with the neurological illness, and why my mother did not get out of bed for days at a time as she used alcohol to cope with her fear and uncertain future. We did not see our mother leave her bed for the hospital, and in an effort to spare us, we were not allowed to visit her. In my mind, she was home one moment and dead the next. No one was home to comfort three young children. I was the oldest, but I did not feel that I had the knowledge or skills to help my younger brothers. No one was there to help me.

In my confused thirteen-year-old mind, I etched a story that would solidify over the next years, as though carved into rock: I did not tell my mother that I loved her that one day, and she died without me ever telling her that she was loved. As a young girl and for many years afterward, I thought I could have saved my mother's life if I had not been so selfish, if I had just given her the little affection she wanted. In my limited, self-centered view of the world, I—rather than illness—had caused her death.

No one spoke about her death, what caused it, or how she died. I did not know what caused her to die. Only after her death did I find a newspaper article tucked away in her jewelry case that described the rare diagnosis of Guillain-Barré syndrome. I could not risk asking questions or sharing my pain for fear that exposing my grief would bring a tsunami of pain to my father. I was afraid that the rest of my family might die too, but talking about or showing my grief would mean rocking the boat and risking whatever stability was left in my life. I did not have words for what I was feeling. I had not seen anyone live through grief, and I did not know if I could survive the pain of what I was feeling. I was alone with my grief, and I could not understand how deeply my misinterpretation of her unexpected death would wound me for a long, long time.

I asked to go back to school just three days later, hoping I could hide in the routine of classes and my commitment to good grades. I did not know any others my age who had lost a parent, and I felt humiliated by the looks of pity and the whispers around me. No one knew what to say, and everyone was visibly uncomfortable around me. I was embarrassed, thinking they could see my inner anguish, ashamed that my feelings made me naked. But one classmate wrote me a note, and to this day, I will never forget her courageous act of reaching out and how her simple words—*I'm sorry about your mother; you must feel so lost*—comforted me in a way my mother would have if she had survived. My young friend risked saying the wrong thing, as we are all afraid we might, in order to acknowledge my new world that I was trying so desperately to navigate.

The greatest act of kindness and compassion would have been for someone to ask me "What do you need to know?" and then encourage an open, ongoing discussion of the facts and my feelings. *What happened? When did she die? What caused her death? Who was with her? Was it my fault?* I needed information to sort through the reality of her death. I needed someone who could explain what happened so I did not fill in the blanks with my worst fantasies. In the absence of real information, I believed she had died alone. I believed I could have stopped it. I believed I was to blame.

I did not know how to speak about my feelings. I needed someone to give me the language of grief and to help me figure out what to do with my confusion, anger, guilt, regret, and overwhelming sadness. I needed an adult to check my assumptions, beliefs, and conclusions, so that I could begin to deal with the reality and start the work of expressing my feelings. I needed someone to listen to me without judgment, to listen to the same stories repeatedly until I came to accept the reality of losing the most important touchstone in a young girl's life. I needed a place to put my grief and a way to externalize it so my body would not implode. I wish now that someone had given me a journal and encouraged me to explore this mysterious new world on paper, to make my questions and beliefs visible to me so that I might at least find words or images that could serve as a lifesaver to hang on to. I needed to know what healthy grieving looked like, and the adults around me did not show me. My father hid his grief inside his bedroom walls, thinking he was protecting us. But I saw his reddened eyes many mornings and wished that we could have cried together.

I vowed to make meaning from my mother's death. I promised myself, *I will not be a victim, and this will not be a tragedy.* In order to cope, I reasoned, some good must come from this. This drive to right a wrong, to untangle my confusion, led me to learn everything I could about dying well and "good grief."

I could not be there for my mother, and my grief reflected that regret. I would use the rest of my life to make sure it would not happen again. I would learn everything I could about what a dying person needs; I would be with others as they were dying. I would study everything I could about healthy grief so others would not be alone and confused in their bereavement, as I had been. I would learn what I had not known so I could support others.

One of my greatest teachers came in the form of an accident, an experience that changed my assumptions and beliefs. When I was twenty-nine years old, I came to know death from the inside looking out. I had a classic near-death experience during a routine dental procedure. I lost consciousness from a reaction to nitrous oxide while in the dentist's chair. The incident changed my assumptions about life, death, and consciousness, and it gave me a sense of peace about death and around others who were dying.

My personal experience with death reinforced my conviction to assist others who were dying, companioning them like a midwife. I also believed I could help their loved ones experience a gentler, healthier grief. So I worked in several hospices around the country as we moved frequently for my husband's job. I sat with over five hundred people as they died, and they told me what mattered to them. In 1994, I formalized my study of death, dying, and grief by returning to a doctoral program and specializing in thanatology, the study of death and dying. I also worked with children in a pediatric AIDS ward who taught me about their lack of fear and acceptance of after-death communication. I spoke at conferences and within university programs trying to dispel the myths and fears of death, and teaching others how to care for the dying and the bereaved.

All of this may sound like noble work, but I now know that it was a self-serving quest. I never again wanted to be unprepared. I wanted to be ready and able to respond during what I knew would eventually come: my father's death. I wanted to manage my lack of control, to bring comfort to my own discomfort. I never again wanted to feel the regret of not responding or not being able to care for a loved one who was dying.

So in July 2003, when my father told me that he had stage IV lung cancer, I felt ready. I had been preparing for this journey since my mother's death. The gaping wound of her death had left an ugly scar, so my healing was to learn enough about death and dying so that I could respond and change the experience from a tragedy into an opportunity to serve and love.

I knew I would respond immediately and commit fully to assisting my father. I knew this was the opportunity for which I had studied and worked my whole life. I canceled the Death & Dying courses I was teaching at the university and closed my private psychotherapy practice. I told my father I would fly to him in Hawaii within days, and I told my husband I would be gone for several months.

Friends asked me if I was afraid. No, I responded. My hospice patients had taught me well, and I could use their gifts to be a witness, a companion, an advocate, and a midwife during my father's dying. I knew it was my privilege to respond to his needs. Allowing me to help him was his gift to me as well my last gift to him.

Unlike during my mother's death, I now had a toolkit of skills, competencies, and information. I had my conviction to be present with him, no matter how painful his illness became. I would not let my grief overshadow his needs, but I also would not separate him from the intimacy of my feelings. My promise to both of us was to be his companion so he would not feel alone and dead before his time. I imagined myself the safe haven, the cocoon, where he could go into metamorphosis and emerge into his next adventure.

I went to him with my belief that there is no right way to die; there is only each person's wish. In death, as in life, each person gets one vote. My guiding principle would be: one life, one death, one vote. I did not have the right to usurp his vote and take away the power of choice about how he lived and how he died. None of us has the right to impose a formula, a prescription, or an agenda for our version of another's good death. He was fortunate enough to be given some time to plan; he had the lucidity, the resources, and the support to follow through with his wishes. I would help him to be the author of his death, as he had been author of his life.

I began our daily rituals to soothe his discomforts. We reviewed his life in stories and scrapbooks; I asked him about the highlights of his life and what he believed his legacy would be. I asked him what he wanted to do before he died and helped him write his bucket list, planning excursions to complete his wishes. We wrote his obituary and talked about where to spread his ashes. I arranged visits for the friends he wanted to see and served as timekeeper to gently escort them out when I sensed he was tired. Each night I massaged and moisturized his cracked, thin skin. I took him to his doctor's appointments and asked the questions that he would not because he was of the generation that often defers to medical authorities. I clarified what the doctor said, and I made sure Dad understood. And when the doctor suggested daily chemotherapy, I asked what my father would not: "What might be the pain, and what will he gain?" Dad decided that the discomfort of traveling and the potential side effects were not worth the extra two weeks of living it might afford him. "You can have what you want," I promised. And so I took him home and arranged for hospice services.

I made his breakfasts; we read the newspaper and talked about the news. I engaged him in subjects and activities in which he was interested, and I watched over him when he was tired. I answered the phone and tended to people he no longer wished to connect with. I offered him options and supported his choices. I asked him, "Do you want to talk about the cancer?" and "What have we not talked about?" He became weaker each day; he was a skeleton of the man I had known all my life, but his presence was still larger than life. I was surprised at what changed each day and how quickly. Neither of us knew what might happen next.

Twelve days after I arrived, he had little appetite but said he wanted Hawaiian food for dinner. He nibbled but was agitated and restless.

I gave him some of the morphine that the hospice had left for him, and we went through our routine of lotion and massage, a talk about our day together, and a goodnight kiss. I stayed by his side like a sentry in case he woke disoriented from the medication.

When he woke up the next morning, he grabbed at the oxygen tube running to his nose, connecting life to his shriveling lungs. He pulled the tube out and slid the strap off from around his head.

"Dad, you need the oxygen," I said.

Firmly and succinctly, he responded, "No more."

I checked my understanding and said, "Dad, if you take out the oxygen tubes, you will die soon. Is that what you want?"

"No more," he repeated.

I was sure, because we had spoken directly about his wishes. He did not want to live a life void of adventure and choice. He did not want to be a burden, and he was ready to go. This was the last choice he could make, and my gift was to support him, rather than to challenge him. I was there to be with him as he pushed off on his last voyage.

I put the tube on the floor and turned the oxygen off. I curled up next to him, cradled his head, and spoke softly to him: "I love you. Thank you. I will never forget you." Softly and gently, and with a lot of space between these truths, I repeated what I needed to send him off with. I sang a favorite Hawaiian song. His eyes were closed. His breathing was slow and shallow for an hour as he lay in my arms. There was a light breeze with the scent of plumeria.

Suddenly, his eyes opened fully. He stared, without blinking, up into the corner of the ceiling. I followed his eyes and heard him whisper, "Duchess," his nickname for my mother. I whispered back, "Yes. It's her. Of course she is here. Go to her. We will be okay. You can go now, Dad." His eyes closed. And within a few minutes, his breathing stopped.

I sobbed and sank down onto his chest. In that moment, I was selfish and wanted him back. In truth, I was thinking only of myself. I had thought I was prepared; I had rehearsed what this moment might be like, but in truth, we are never ready and we always want more time with someone we love. And then in the next moment, I remembered what I had seen and what I knew to be true. I knew where he was; I knew he was whole and healed; I knew he was not alone. I knew, too, that I was not alone. Love trumps death.

I had done what I came to do. I could not change his mortality, but I made a difference during his dying, as he had made a difference all my life. I could not save him, but I shared and participated in his dying, as I had in his life. I responded and contributed compassion. Remembering my part in his dying heals my grief and continues to sustain me.

I share my story with you and hope that you, too, will be able to offer your loved one the death of his or her choice and to honor their values right up to the end of their life. We all want to make a positive difference in each other's lives, but we often feel powerless and do not know how to help. I hope the information and stories that follow will empower you to dispel your fears and your loved one's anxieties, raising your confidence around illness, death, and grief. I hope you will respond to a loved one's needs so that your experience of service is what you are left with, rather than regret. My wish for you is that in the end, you feel gratitude rather than grief, and love rather than loss.

1

HOW WE DIE MATTERS

I've told my children that when I die, to release balloons in the sky to celebrate that I graduated. For me, death is a graduation.
ELISABETH KÜBLER-ROSS, PSYCHIATRIST, PIONEER IN DEATH STUDIES, AND
AUTHOR OF *ON DEATH AND DYING*

Attitudes are the feelings, thoughts, perspectives, and postures toward death and dying, illness and disease that affect how we respond to end-of-life matters. Those feelings and thoughts are taught. The positions are positive, negative, or neutral. Family, society, peers, and influential role models indoctrinate us. We can be taught that death is normal and natural, or we can be taught that it is to be avoided and ignored. We can understand death as a transition, a change, and a graduation or as an end, a punishment, or a judgment. What we are taught and the model of care we are shown will affect how we live in the world, side by side with the reality of death. We will either make friends with death, accepting it as a part of life, or we will deny its power and potential to teach us how to live.

Our experiences of illness and dying have everything to do with what we believe, and our belief is dependent on what we perceive. Our perception is based on our perspective, or the way we see the world, as a result of our attitudes. Illness may lessen our physical strength or deny us of physical abilities and roles, but our attitudes can narrow or enlarge how we experience reality. Our attitudes and expectations impact how we experience living and dying, rather than the circumstances surrounding our living or our dying.

If you are approaching death, you have more options and opportunities to experience your dying in more ways than you previously believed or were told. If you change the way you perceive dying, the drama and anguish will soften. You can be left with time to use toward loving and experiencing peace. You can die with grace and gratitude, finding peace before death rather than after it.

Dying Well Has to Do with Managing Our Fears

Our fears and anxieties are barriers to compassionate care, stemming from our attitudes, assumptions, lack of experience, and lack of knowledge. The fear says, "I cannot handle (some part of) dying."

The barrier has developed as a result of prolific social and technological changes in the last two hundred years. The secularization of society, the dominance of science within medical practices, and the pressure of population expansion have affected people's attitudes and behaviors about death and dying. Death used to be a family and community experience in the villages of rural America; family members and friends attended to the dying at home and made personal preparations for disposal of the body. The reality of death was cushioned by the emotional and social support of an extended family network and meaningful rituals.

As Western society moved from a religious orientation to a perspective dominated by the values of science, trade, and business, the management of the dying patient shifted from the family to a team of professionals. Death, expelled from the common experiences of everyday life, became more of an unknown and mysterious factor of life. In the nineteenth century, death was a prominent aspect of family discussion and responsibility; family members were cared for and died at home, and then they were laid out in the central parlor for visitations. Today the reality of death is hidden, unspoken, and de-ritualized. People's direct experience with death and dying as a natural human transition has decreased drastically. As a result, they have fewer opportunities to learn how to handle themselves or help others during illness and through death. More people die in hospitals and nursing homes rather than in the comfort of their own home, and yet research reveals that 90 percent of people want to stay at home to die.[1]

How a loved one dies is important to the patient as well as the family and caregivers. A striking study reported in a 2010 issue of the *Journal of Clinical Oncology* found that bereaved caregivers of patients who died in an intensive care unit of a hospital were five times more likely to be diagnosed with post-traumatic stress disorder (PTSD), compared with caregivers of patients who died at home with hospice services.[2] End-of-life care in hospitals differs from hospice care that emphasizes pain management and quality of life. Families of patients who died in the hospital, though not in an intensive care unit, also were at risk for manifesting an intense and disabling form of grief.

The mission of the current death awareness movement is to neutralize fear and normalize the process of dying. The work of Dame Cicely Saunders of England and Dr. Elisabeth Kübler-Ross in the United States, both physicians and writers, taught the public about the normal reactions to death and the needs of dying patients. Kübler-Ross taught professionals how to cope with death, to assist others in understanding the process of dying, and to effectively intervene in the emotional, physical, spiritual, and social concerns preceding death. In turn, both physicians worked to advance the hospice movement and to increase the public's awareness of and interest in the dying process, death, and grief. They emphasized the importance of palliative comfort care for the dying and taught us how to assist during illness and dying. The field of death education and counseling was developed to offer alternative perspectives and solutions to the complex needs in a changing society.

However, death education must compete with other requirements of professional preparation. There is serious competition for the funds, resources, time, and opportunity to offer specialized instruction in schools of nursing, medicine, pharmacy, and social work. Empirical evidence shows that novice counselors feel severely limited in skills when presented with clients' issues of grief, impending death, and life-threatening illness. Though most professional schools currently provide some education in death and dying, most do not offer an entire course. In the most common program, which offers one or two lectures, students receive a superficial and limited exposure to the subject.

Several professional organizations have been formed to promote research and communication between disciplines and memberships. The Association for Death Education and Counseling (ADEC) and the International Work Group (IWG) on Death, Dying, and Bereavement encourage and promote the death awareness movement. Both groups are nonprofit, educational, professional, and scientific organizations devoted to the promotion and upgrade of death education and death-related counseling. The field of death education and counseling, the hospice movement, and the death awareness movement were developed to offer alternative perspectives and solutions to complex needs in a changing world.

A positive outcome of these movements would be that societies are able to approach dying consciously, to accept it as a natural process, and to become more comfortable with the reality of death. That comfort and acceptance becomes our ultimate goal because it means more peace and less fear during our dying. Acceptance will bring more resources, knowledge, and support to dying people, their families, and those participating in the process. It will serve to bring death into the open and away from being taboo. Reducing our fears and increasing our competency may help those people who want to die in their homes, and especially those who want to live right up to the end of their lives the way they choose.

Dying Well Has More to Do with Our Conversations

The healing that we most want may come not from medical interven-tion or technology but from meaningful human contact and kindness. A common complaint I have heard from dying patients is "My dying is lonely, and I need to talk, but everyone avoids the subject." Repeated studies of terminally ill patients revealed that they were most concerned with being abandoned or rejected by significant people in their lives, losing control or the ability to manage their lives, and being in over-whelming pain or distress. Conversations can address each of these common concerns because we hear the dying person's experience, accept and validate his needs, companion him without usurping his control, and use information to address his distress.

The conversations that bring us together against the loneliness of dying are the conversations that reflect our humanity:

- What do you value?
- How do you want to die?
- With whom do you want to spend your last moments?
- If it were up to you, when might it be time to quit?
- Whom can you count on?
- What do you leave as your legacy?

These conversations help dying people live their lives on their terms and according to their values, connect them with meaningful others, and assist them in finishing the business of living.

However, these conversations can be difficult for most people. Families and friends as well as physicians are reluctant to initiate dis-cussion about the patient's prognosis or end-of-life options, but the conversations are crucial if our loved one is to receive the care and live her life in accordance with her values. As caregivers, we can inform and advocate for our loved one, offering her hospice care and options such as palliative care that will ease her pain and anxiety as she approaches her death.

When we have honest, direct conversations about end-of-life choices, people are more likely to receive the end-of-life care they desire. With information from these conversations, caregivers and family members are more comfortable, knowledgeable, and participative in the processes of dying and grieving. A consumer might perceive the final "product" as a conscious and peaceful death. The patient and family would accept less aggressive treatment with less stress and more quality of life. The survivor would realize less guilt, greater peace, and less complicated grief. In the short term, medical intervention and heroic measures may prolong a fragile life, but there is a long-range perspective that impacts generations to come.

The person who is dying can design his death by communicating his wishes as though his vision, needs, and requests were his art. This art is the intentional expression of his life values, and these values continue until the moment of death. Framing these values is like spotlighting what the dying person wants to focus upon, and it helps demonstrate his personal power and freedom over as much as possible. Death will happen, *but how death happens* and *how the dying person reacts* are still within his power.

As caregivers, how we intervene with our most vulnerable loved ones today leaves a legacy for generations to come. Lessons become beacons on the horizon, building generations with character development, values of kindness and compassion, and the essential qualities that make us most humane. We have an important opportunity to educate and model conscious dying and conscientious service in order to shape the next generation's ability to care for one another. It is as though we can provide a disaster relief program through the landmines of dying if we will begin having honest conversations between the dying and the caregivers, between the elderly and the youth, between those being diagnosed and those in remission from disease.

When we intervene, we model and teach others how they too can make a difference and be of service. The changes we demonstrate because of new attitudes, knowledge, skills, and experience lead to a *death competency* that means we have a willingness to complete death preparation tasks.[3] Death-related skills include actions such as preparing a will, making decisions about organ donation and funeral preparations, and listening to the concerns of a dying patient. It means that people have the ability and willingness to respond to challenges introduced by death and dying.

But instead, too many deaths are missed opportunities. We do not assist in the process of living-up-to-death that is possible because we resist looking at the mystery and sacredness of dying. We do not inquire; we do not talk; we do not share our experiences. And so we do not educate and empower each other. We do not accept the reality of what is right in front of us and lift the veil of our illusions and fears that keeps us from one another. That separation and fear is our suffering, and it feeds the guilt after our loved one has died. Instead, we can approach the mystery of death as our deepest inquiry and with a posture of a child's mind—we can investigate, wonder, observe without judgment, holding back nothing, with a heart wide open. We can be fully present with death, and then we can be of service to our loved one.

Five Lasting Breaths to Honor the Relationship

What you may need to say before your loved one dies:

- I love you.
- Thank you.
- Please forgive me.

- I forgive you.
- It's okay to go.

❧ ❧ ❧

Dying Well Has More to Do with Transforming a Relationship

Assisting a loved one in dying well means that we steward well. We serve well, without judging how our loved one is changing under the burden of disease or while she is showing fear of the unknown. We can help her die well without trying to change the inevitable. We can model acceptance for her journey and the choices she is able to make. We do not have to understand her choices in order to accept them; we need only choose to accept from our heart and let go of our need to understand from our head. The inevitability of death may finally teach us that we cannot control anything except our attitude. And the only attitude that matters when facing death is acceptance and love. That position changes the experience of death from one of fearful isolation to one of loving connection.

Dying Well Can Enhance the Emotional Bond

Death changes a relationship, but it need not end it. A relationship is an association, a connection, a link, and a tie between loved ones. We can continue to be in a relationship with our loved one even after their death, even in spite of his or her physical absence.

In my case, I believe and act in a way that reflects that I am still my father's daughter long after his death. I maintain the identity of daughter through my behavior and ways that I maintain that role. I continue to act as his daughter. Daughter can be both a noun and a verb. I behave in ways that demonstrate that I am not finished being his daughter.

I extend myself to his friends, attend to the charities he cared about, and maintain the values he cherished. A relationship is about caregiving, and it is part of my grief recovery to create opportunities to care for the people, beliefs, and values as he would, in his stead. The legacy of his values and what I do with that legacy is an ongoing gift that links me to him and maintains his presence in my life today.

With that attitude we can look for ways that our loved one made a difference in the community. We can look for ways to maintain his values through projects, to carry out anonymous acts of kindness, and to continue to participate in activities that we enjoyed together. It is empowering to maintain a relationship with him, no matter how private or invisible. It is personal, real, and meaningful. The emotional bond is intact and strong even after death.

Dying well is a triumph of love over the specter of death—what is left after the person is gone is the meaning of the relationship and the survivors that are left holding the love for that person. Dying well is about knowing the physical relationship will change through death, but the bond of love transcends death. We are human beings who seek meaning and people to love; helping our loved one die well reconciles both needs.

A transforming relationship means we can learn to carry our deceased loved one in a new way. We learn, through trial and error, how to weave our loved one and her values into this new life without her. We create a new life that evokes the memories, values, and ethics of our loved one, live in a new way with her in a different world, and relate to her memory in a new way. But we are always, through love, in a relationship with her.

Helping our loved ones to die well matters, because it may be our last opportunity to be of service and to share love with our loved one. Dying provides us an advantageous chance to be open and accept the realities of our finiteness. I know that service through the dying process matters, to both the dying person and the surviving family members. We can learn to thrive in the midst of the pain and anguish of letting go. We can continue loving in spite of the pain and cost of losing a loved one. There is a ripple effect when we offer comfort and enrichment to the dying; that person affects the experience of the dying person, and their own grief during and after their loved one's death, and impacts future generations by showing the best of humanity.

Actions to Honor the Relationship

- Spend time naming what your loved one means to you; memorialize him while he is alive and can appreciate your thanksgiving.
- Talk about the elephant in the room. If your loved one knows she is dying and talks about her impending death directly or indirectly, acknowledge the truth and address her experience. To not follow her where she wants to go is to ignore her in her greatest need.
- However, in the same way, respect a person's need for denial. If he chooses to ignore his circumstances or diagnosis, he has the right to proceed to his death in his own way and timing. As we discuss the diagnosis or prognosis of the disease, I might say to him, "If you ask me a question, I will tell you the truth," indicating I will respect his direction and follow his lead.
- Stay in your heart instead of in your head. Stay in the present instead of in the future. Try to stop projecting and rehearsing the death; often it is our way of protecting ourselves, but it takes us away from being with our loved one.
- Always behave as though the person who is in a coma, who is unconscious or nonresponsive, can hear you.

Hearing is the last of the senses to go, so speak to your loved one and say what is important.

- Use a soft voice to be sensitive to the fragility of hearing at the end stage. Use a normal, respectful tone.
- Words are not the only source of communication. Sometimes the most authentic way of connecting is through touch, a genuine smile, a gentle stroke that says, "I love you. I am with you."

Notes

1. Marilyn J. Field and Christine K. Cassel, eds., *Approaching Death: Improving Care at the End of Life* (Washington, DC: The National Academies Press, 1997), 33–49.

Mary Sheppard and Meredith Levine, "A Good Death: About This Series," *CBC News* (May 13, 2011), http://www.cbc.ca/news/health/story/2011/05/04/f-milestogo-project-overview.html.

2. Alexi A. Wright et al., "Place of Death: Correlations with Quality of Life of Patients with Cancer and Predictors of Bereaved Caregivers' Mental Health," *Journal of Clinical Oncology* (September 13, 2010).

3. Rosemary A. Robbins, "Death Competency: Bugen's Coping with Death Scale and Death Self-Efficacy," in *Death Anxiety Handbook*, ed. Robert A. Neimeyer (Washington, DC: Taylor & Francis, 1994), 149–65.

2

WE CAN MAKE A DIFFERENCE

Any undivided attention is prayer.
SIMONE WEIL, FRENCH PHILOSOPHER AND
AUTHOR OF *GRAVITY AND GRACE*

People with illness feel judged when others project thoughts like *He did not pray enough* or *She was not an exceptional cancer patient.* We will all succumb to death. Death does not catch us. We can never try hard enough or pray long enough or know enough to get out of this life alive. We cannot control the inevitability of death, but we can have an impact on how we think about our death, how we respond to illness, and how present we are with our dying loved ones.

Only our thoughts, choices, and actions toward dying are within our control. When we choose helpful attitudes and thoughts, we can make a significant difference in the process of how our loved ones die. Those thoughts may not always be hopeful in the ways that deny the realism of disease, but we can see beyond the limits of the body and the fears of the moment. Those attitudes can discern the mystery and the mystical, the complexity and simplicity of love and kindness. As Antoine de Saint-Exupéry wrote, "What is essential is invisible to the eye."

Our can-do culture believes in its omnipotence, similar to the way we believe in the immortality of youth. We feed ourselves the fantasy that we can control, monitor, slow, and ultimately avert death. Our culture often defines death as a result of personal error or defeat. It is easier to avoid our feelings surrounding death when naming a dying patient by a clinical study, room number, or surgical procedure. Judgments are indirect, ubiquitous, and subconscious; they are hidden in the media, in music, and in the ways that we teach or don't teach our youth. The pervasive message is "If we die, we are to blame." The impression is that we have failed. We have lost the natural rhythms and cycles of life because so much is now manipulated, augmented, and designed to suit our limited framework of right and wrong.

Death is transition. Death is change. It is we who judge and label illness, dying, and death. The problem is not death; death happens. Death is a reality. Dying becomes a problem depending on how we think about it and respond to it. How different our experience of dying, death, and grief would be if we could view dying with a clarity that knows it as change and transition—a clarity that doesn't judge. How different our experience would be if we believed that death is a transition rather than an end, a graduation instead of an expulsion, a going home rather than a black hole of oblivion, that it offers us opportunities for growth rather than strips us of everything.

Can we begin to question our past assumptions about death, illness, and grief? Is death the end of a person or an end to the feelings of love? Is death always a tragedy? Is death a failure of the living? Is death a failure at all?

I am most comforted by a particular line in Walt Whitman's poem "Song of Myself": "All goes onward and outward, nothing collapses, / And to die is different from what any one supposed, and luckier." What if death is not the tragedy? What if *how* we die is far more painful than any illness? What if our ideas of death are only a story, and not the ending we fear?

The language around death makes illness and dying all the more difficult to manage. We use words and euphemisms about death that reflect our judgment, comparison, and fear that in turn close us off from one another at a time we most need connection and reassurance. When we say someone kicked the bucket, bit the dust, gave up the ghost, or is collateral damage, we are often unaware of our defensiveness and need to minimize our discomfort, deny the reality, and protect our feelings. A person's language helps shape his reality of death. How we speak about death and our feelings affects what we think and how we experience death, dying, and grief.

Death Is Universal and Inevitable

All living things will die. Death happens to everyone; it is what we all have in common. It connects us, gives us our humanness, and when we share our commonality of grief, death teaches us empathy. No one is absolved of death. No one who loves escapes grief. Death cannot be avoided. It happens every minute of every day and in every part of the planet, and it is not happening to only you and your loved one, though it may feel like you are very alone and this is the most devastating of all deaths.

Even if we cannot stop the decay or the dying, we can enter into the process rather than turn away. We can ultimately honor the sacred dimensions of our loved one and our relationship. We can ask to be allowed to serve and witness, rather than give up and be absent. We must keep the big picture before us, that what we are ultimately doing is communicating and sharing love, so right through to the end of her life, our loved one experiences peace rather than fear. We can tend to the invisible and most significant pain reported by terminally ill patients, the pain of isolation and loneliness; that is a suffering beyond the pain that science can alleviate. We can comfort when it matters most, through our presence and simple acts of kindness and humanity: touching, listening, attending, and helping the dying to find meaning and leave a legacy.

We can be of service during our loved one's dying and death. Our active and intentional participation in our loved one's dying is love in action. It is more than a reply; it is a response. Some might avoid it, deny it, diminish its import, minimize the opportunity, and let the moments pass by. If we acknowledge the inevitability of death and fully participate in these moments of life, we may be more alive than most others ever experience. We may give each other permission to be fully vulnerable and available as we have never been before. I can't remember who said, "It is possible to be alive but mostly dead in the world of the living . . . or dying but feeling alive for the first time," but it rings true. If we knew we could make a difference, we would never turn away. We would not give up, and there would be no reason to give up. *How* we help them get to the end matters.

As family and friends of a dying loved one, we can each make a difference in our own unique way. You might imagine that we are all playing different instruments in the orchestra at the end of life. Each of us adds to the symphony; we may come in at different times in the music, use different instruments, play at different levels of competency, but we all play together to assist our loved one with what is needed. We play the best we can with the skills and the energy we have in the moment.

Each person's participation is helpful and works together to form a net that supports the dying and the family through this life-changing journey. The point is not to do it perfectly but to participate to the fullest of our ability. My family's involvement with my father's care was collaborative and like a symphony. Our communal efforts made a difference to my father's experience of dying and to our experience with our grief. Our memories, now eight years after his death, continue to be some of the strongest and most tender ties between us.

How Service Matters

1. Participation and communication reduce the sense of isolation for the patient during dying. Persons who are actively dying, or know of

their terminal diagnosis, report that what they fear more than physical pain or the finality of death is their sense of being abandoned. Most feel that their emotions and the issues they are facing are ignored. Connection with them softens their experience of isolation and comforts body, mind, and spirit.

2. When family or friends participate in caregiving, patients report less fear of dying, which leads to a greater capacity for experiencing the time that is left. Patients experience increased appreciation in life, acceptance of the time they have lived, and feelings of peace in the present.

3. When you act as a caregiver, you experience a reduced sense of helplessness during a loved one's illness and death, which leads to less guilt, remorse, anxiety, and complicated grief during illness and after death. A caregiver is thus more able to express that she did what she could to demonstrate her tenderness, love, and respect for the dying person.

4. Everyone realizes increased choices from a more informed position; there are greater resources, including a connection to others with similar challenges. Patients, caregivers, and family all experience that they are not alone and that death is a universal condition.

5. We can strengthen communication with our dying loved one; we can achieve a cohesive, honest, and open communication within families.

6. All involved report a heightened sense of competency from new skills, training, and awareness.

7. There can be a greater sense of peace in the midst of life's greatest challenge.

❧ ❧ ❧

The Caregiver's Prayer

I ask that you give me the strength and the compassion to stay the course, so that I might make friends with death and not look away from my loved one.

❧ ❧ ❧

Support Your Dying Loved One's Values and Choices

There is no one right way to die. There is no best death. If we were given a choice, it would be the personal journey and reflection of our values. Given a choice, some people's preference might be a quick death during their sleep; they might want to avoid pain at all costs. Others value the opportunity to say good-bye to loved ones, so they would prefer the time that heart disease might allow them, even if pain accompanied that time. Both choices are aligned with the individual's values and, as such, are right for him or her.

There is no one-death-fits-all model. Death is a complex mystery, unique to each individual. We may be able to diagnose the cause of death, estimate a trajectory of time remaining, and map the disease in the body, but there is no formula for a perfect death. Each death is as unique as the individual; each trail toward death is as exceptional as a fingerprint.

The best model of care we can offer will center on the person rather than on her disease and will focus on the life she has remaining. We will not view our loved one as damaged, diseased, disorganized, or incompetent; not as someone who needs to be fixed, but as someone further along the journey of life with whom we have the privilege of being present.

Our goal should be to help facilitate the way of dying that our loved one envisions, that is consistent and congruent with his personal values. We can help the dying identify, communicate, and live his values. Most often, we assume that we know what our loved ones want and need, and we don't inquire. We impose our needs and values onto others. It is not our place, or our right, to facilitate the kind of death we would want when it's not our death. We must ask open-ended questions about what he cares about, values, believes, and needs. We must step back from our personal needs, wants, and agendas. We must see and hear what is needed. And then we must paraphrase his request to clarify our observations and what we have heard. Then we can act with the intention of serving as our loved one wishes to be served.

How to Make a Difference

- Support your dying loved one's values and choices.
- Make no assumptions.
- Censor any judgment.
- Make no comparisons.
- Let go of the need to *understand* his choices; instead, choose to *accept* his choices.
- Give your dying loved one as much control as possible.
- Advocate for your dying loved one's self-determination.
- Ask what your dying loved one needs and respond appropriately.
- Attend to your dying loved one's practical needs.
- Attend to your dying loved one's emotional and spiritual needs.
- Find your caregiver role.

❦ ❧ ❦

Make No Assumptions

Do not assume that this person is experiencing what you are going through or that she needs what you think you might if you were in her situation. We must not presume to know what she is thinking, feeling, or needing in any moment. Do not expect that what was needed yesterday is the same today.

Attend to her as though you were just getting to know her, without any agenda, history, or past assumptions. For example, when it was my job to visit day after day with the same patients in a hospital, before I went into each person's room, I would pause and visualize myself taking a shower to wash away any knowledge or preconceptions I had about that person that I may have developed from the previous visits. Such an exercise gave me the humility to enter with an attitude of openness and without blinders from any preconceptions. Be open and flexible, and let her set the course.

Disease, decline, and dying are about daily loss and, often, unwilling surrender. Over time, the dying person surrenders his abilities, roles, strength, independence, and sense of control. He loses his health and vigor, privacy and mobility, and dreams for the future. When so much is slipping away beyond his grasp, we can give back his power and self-esteem by suggesting options rather than dictating mandates, and by guiding rather than pushing.

Censor Any Judgment

A dying person's values, choices, and decisions should be honored. Judgment and prejudice on the caregivers' part indicate a need for control, a belief that we know what is best. It is arrogant to believe that we can know more than we do. Our challenge is to fully observe, from an objective, detached, witness state, where we are strong enough to welcome everything and push away nothing. At this time, dying is not our journey, and the related decisions are not ours to make. This does not mean we will like everything that is happening, but it is not our right to approve or disapprove. Our opportunity is to honor and respond to our loved one's values. In order to respond to the changing landscape of disease and dying, we must get out of our own way and discover, with open hearts, how our loved one wants to move toward her end.

Universal Protocol for Care of the Dying

- Be nonjudgmental. This is the time to put your beliefs, values, and opinions in silence mode so you can affirm and support the person for whom you are caring. Do not use words such as *should, ought to,* or *why,* which often suggest judgment or second-guessing. Treat the person with dignity and respect despite her history or reactions to her illness.

- Listen and respond from the heart. The process of dying is unique to each individual and often a mystery. His illness and his dying are not problems to be fixed. You may have feelings about difficult moments, but maintain your focus on the dying person and do not ask him to help you work through your grief or to comfort you.

- Let the dying person be your teacher. The patient is the expert during this journey. Do not pretend to be the expert on her culture, faith, or illness. Do not take over.

Make No Comparisons

Each disease is complex and complicated, intricate and always changing. The same is true about your loved one. It is hurtful, not helpful, to compare and contrast your loved one or his disease and how it is progressing to anyone else's situation. Allow him an *authentic death*. Do not raise the bar and hold him up to unrealistic standards that are out of character. Do not elevate the dying to heroic statures ... it separates him from real loved ones and diminishes his humanity. Do not set expectations for heroics. The most heroic thing patients can do is face the reality of dying with as much as they can bring to the table. Likewise, caregivers and family members are heroic when they look death in the face and are fully present. The disease is as complex, unique, and mysterious as the person. Respect both.

Let go of the need to *understand* the dying person's choices; instead, choose to *accept* her choices. Your contribution is not in understanding but in accepting and supporting her choices, values, and needs. When most people say, "I don't understand," it is code for "I don't agree" or "I won't go along with that until you convince me." But you are here to honor your loved one's values, support her choices, and help her live the life she can right up to the moment of death. Her agenda, not yours, is of importance. Don't assume ownership over her last decisions.

The deepest, most selfless humanity comes only when we have the discipline and lack of ego to avoid imposing our personal story and needs onto another person. If we are telling our story, we are not seeing our loved one, or truly being with him, but merely using him as a projection of ourselves.

The goal is compassionate detachment, which is very difficult for most people to realize. It means serving another person without imposing our views, biases, or needs on her way of living or dying. Many people mistakenly believe that this is cold and uncaring, without compassion, but to be so respectful of another person's path and life choices is to support her at the highest level.

While serving your dying loved one, make it a spiritual practice to continually ask yourself, *Whose needs am I meeting?* We must rigorously and honestly discern the difference between our own needs, wants, and agenda and our loved one's wishes and needs. We must ask ourselves such things as *Does he need to talk, or is that my need?* or *Do I need friends to visit, or is that his need?* Let his needs and wishes guide you, and be willing to let others, not your dying loved one, help you to take care of your needs.

Give Your Loved One as Much Control as Possible

Let the patient set the tone and pace of the visit. For example, ask permission to sit on the bed, to talk, or to touch. Ask, "Do you feel like talking about what this is like for you?" versus asking probing questions and assuming the person wants to disclose. Asking "Do you feel like having company now?" allows the person to say no without making it personal. Offer choices. For example, ask if she likes being hugged or wants to be touched. Some people might prefer not to be touched because touch interrupts their feelings and moves them to take on the role of the comforter rather than allowing you to comfort them. When touching or holding hands, put your hand *under* your loved one's hand so he has the control to remove or lighten the touch. Be aware that the dying are often afraid of, but longing for, the reassurance of touch because they may feel ugly, old, or a burden to others.

Give the dying sovereignty over her death. This underscores her right and prerogative to have authority over the entire course of her life, up to the moment of death, if that is possible. Demonstrate a genuine care and concern for her entire well-being, even if that might be counter to your wishes or perspective. We should not dominate our loved one, even when she is frail or in need; we cannot exploit her condition or dictate from our personal agenda; we must not intrude or invade when we think her decision is wrong, even during illness.

Some may choose comfort over cure or resist extreme options in favor of slow medicine like hospice care. My father was clear and vocal about not calling an ambulance for any reason and that he not be taken to the hospital. He was adamant that he did not want to die surrounded by machines and professionals. He preferred to die sooner and at home rather than to live longer, only to be cared for by strangers. Even if it meant we would have had him in our lives months longer in the hospital with treatment, we would not have sacrificed his values and his view of quality of life in favor of our needs.

Advocate for Your Dying Loved One's Self-Determination

Maintain the dying person's freedom and self-management for as long as possible. Believe in his expertise in his own life. Reflect back to him his abilities and competencies. Encourage him by being a nurturer for as long as possible rather than taking away responsibilities, tasks, and independence. Illness does not mean he is now deaf, blind, or incompetent. The effects of physical decline, illness, and aging do not mean we should speak to our loved one in a childish voice or with inflections that suggest he is less intelligent or responsible. Do not assume that he cannot hear you or does not understand if he does not respond; rather, the end of life is the time when he is withdrawing physically, emotionally, and operationally from his environment and relationships. Take the stance that he is doing the work of this phase of life as his body shuts down and his spirit prepares for transition. Respect his withdrawal and the ways he is preparing to die. Do not treat him as an infant, but do respect the fragile state of all his senses and speak softly, touch gently, and limit any harsh sounds, scents, sensations, and movement from his environment. As illness progresses, strength and mobility most likely diminish and your role as caregiver grows, but before assuming that position, ask and make objective observations of your loved one.

Ask What Your Dying Loved One Needs

1. How can I support you and your end-of-life decisions? Who do you want included in the discussions? Who do you most trust with your physical care? With financial matters? With legal decisions? To make arrangements after your death?

2. What kind of care do you want for yourself if you are no longer able to make your wishes known, such as if you had a stroke or were in a coma? Do you want a feeding tube, hydration, and pain medication? Do you want to institute do not resuscitate (DNR) orders? (Put these in writing and discuss them with all the primary caregivers. If possible, have a face-to-face meeting with all caregivers present at once so everyone is hearing the same information and you can each check for understanding and agreement.)

3. What are your greatest fears when you think about the end of your life? What do you need in order to relieve those fears?

4. What do you hope for during your last days? Is there someone you want to see or talk to? Is there someplace you want to visit? Can I help you write a letter to someone?

5. If you have a life-threatening illness, such as kidney failure, and the treatments are only making you sicker without curing the disease, will you want me to talk about ending treatment? How can I help you if you still have hope?

Attend to Your Dying Loved One's Practical Needs

The physical needs for a healthy diet, adequate hydration, a safe environment, and safe mobility are primary goals. As caregivers we can tend to the body as a sacred garden, providing the nutrition, water, oxygen, sunlight, touch, and love that are needed to nourish and maintain the field. We can tend to the body by asking our loved one what she is not getting that would help her to feel more comfortable and safe. We can inquire about what is missing from her regular routine of self-care and ask her to imagine what would soothe and relieve her stress. Her physical condition and needs may change day to day, so we need to be observant, open, flexible, and accepting of whatever emerges.

Assess how well he is sleeping. Is anything interfering with a solid night's sleep? Can he get to sleep relatively quickly and stay asleep? If his sleep is interrupted in the middle of the night to go to the bathroom, is he able to get back to sleep quickly? Is his bedroom conducive to sleep without electronic equipment? Is it cool and dark? Is the mattress comfortable and supportive? Ask him what would soothe him to sleep more readily. Would a nightly massage, lotion application for dry skin, a warm bath, soft music, or a book read to him help with the transition to sleep?

Pain management assessment and needs are constantly in flux. We have to differentiate whether pain is emotional, physical, or spiritual. Inquiring about where the pain is felt and the intensity of the pain helps to identify and locate the source of the distress. Helping the dying person attach words or adjectives to the pain can direct us to a solution. The pain may be emotional and have to do with the need for forgiveness and contact with another person with whom she has been estranged. You can address that emotional pain by listening to her talk about the rift or facilitating communication between them. The pain may be more spiritual and existential in nature, such as questioning her relationship with God or wrestling with questions about what happens after death. Or her discomfort might be physical and relieved through massage or stretching exercises.

Often the pain comes from a combination of sources, and it might be labeled phantom pain, or invisible, when it is not detectable. It is important to always validate your loved one's experience of pain and to respond with pain management options. The National Center for Health Statistics indicates that while 20 percent of dying patients in hospitals have severe pain, only a fraction of 1 percent need be in pain.[1] A medical team can assess and recommend pain management options. The field of palliative care medicine addresses the dying person's specific needs for pain control, symptom management, quality of life, and holistic comfort. It is realistic and completely within our capability to relieve the dying of their physical, emotional, and spiritual pain. Pain management should be a vigorously pursued priority.

Medical management is often overwhelming and ever changing. Maintaining an accurate list of the medical team, medications (dosages and refill regimens), and appointments requires someone to keep the list up to date and in one binder. Any changes need to be recorded and checked for accuracy with the medical team. Periodically checking for medication contraindications with a pharmacist is also a good idea, especially when there is a team of doctors without one medical care coordinator.

One person may be the record keeper. Another person may be comfortable and skilled as an advocate and communicator. As an advocate, this person would intervene on your loved one's behalf by attending all appointments, asking questions, interpreting what the medical team reported, and following up in whatever ways are needed. Be cognizant and respectful of your loved one's personality style and values; one person may not want you to speak for him, but another may need you to be the voice that questions. My father was of a generation that did not second-guess a physician, so he would not ask for clarification or for a second opinion, believing that it would be disrespectful.

Knowing this, and asking my father for his permission to intervene on his behalf, I became his advocate and the person who raised questions.

When information and conversation are shared between the dying and her family members and caregivers, it leads to better understanding, increased cooperation, and lower stress for everyone. When your loved one has stated her goals for care, she generally experiences less aggressive intervention, less stress, more resiliency, and higher self-esteem. At the same time, family members realize higher confidence, greater resolution to problems, and less grief.

Are financial records accessible? Are affairs up to date? Have a medical power of attorney and a financial power of attorney been designated, and have they been communicated to family in writing? Are papers where they can be accessed quickly in case of an emergency? For example, in most states, a DNR order is invalid unless it is with the patient at the time of service. If the patient is incoherent or otherwise unable to make his wishes known and does not have written directions, the hospital is obligated to make efforts to arrest death. That means that if the patient is picked up at home by an ambulance and transported to a hospital, he will have to have the legal paperwork with him to avoid unwanted intervention.

Can someone be designated to look out for the children's needs? If the dying person is a young parent whose spouse is involved at the hospital, it would free both of them of worry if someone were tending to the children's school requirements, after-school schedules, bedtime routines, and emotional needs.

It is a great service, but often overlooked, to have someone managing the friends' and community's questions and involvement. We assume they mean well, but at different times of illness and decline, outside interest may require too much energy from your loved one or yourself and may be perceived as an intrusion. Someone close to the family who knows you can differentiate between close, inner-circle friends and family, and peripheral acquaintances, who for their own reasons, want to say good-bye. This person could intervene on the dying person's behalf and suggest that acquaintances—or anyone whom the dying does not have energy to visit with—share their good wishes or say good-bye in ways other than in person.

Attend to Your Dying Loved One's Emotional and Spiritual Needs

Like icebergs, much of our lives are lived below the surface. Our physical needs are the tip of the iceberg, but our emotional, psychological, and spiritual needs may be the more significant ones hiding below the surface.

At the end of our lives, we need intimacy that comes from truth, whatever it is. We need the truth of love, the truth of our relationships, the truth to accept the process of dying. Truth brings connection and participation, but pretending and protecting leave the dying person with loneliness and separation. Dying in isolation and loneliness are what the dying report as their greatest fears, not death itself. Dying patients actually cope better once they are given full information if they ask for the truth about their prognosis and the process of dying. We caregivers need to put our energies into the affirmation of what is real and participate fully, despite the intense pain of inevitable separation.

As caregivers, we want to give our loved one the sure sense that we are fully present with him, that we allow whatever he is experiencing in the moment (whether we understand it or not), and that we validate his feelings. All people need to feel significant and important to another human being; we need our lives to have meaning and purpose. Paying attention to our loved one's attachments and emotional bonds provides a sense of security, safety, well-being, and hope. Being that comforting presence as a caregiver often comes down to the simple act of being present—being the person who sees, knows, accepts, and forgives the dying for all parts of him, including perhaps a difficult death.

Illness and a prognosis of death make up a terribly isolating time of life. For family and friends, the reality of impending death should be our wake-up call to fully enter into a relationship with our loved one. This time of her illness and our caring response constitute an opportunity for both parties. It is her last chance for human touch, meaningful connection, and to know that she matters. She needs to feel a sense of belonging and to be treated as a living, vital person instead of a dying patient or a hospital room number or a disease. It is our last chance with our loved one to give of ourselves and to love unconditionally.

That connection with others is what is often referred to as the heart of healing because it touches what is invisible, inexplicable; it touches the soul. The connection between the dying and the caregiver can touch both hearts; the way we spend our time together on the journey is our soul work and leaves us both healed in invisible, inexplicable ways.

For the dying person, knowing that he matters is vital. Knowing that his life was of value and that he contributed will make up his legacy, giving him a sense of immortality. It has been suggested that some people are more afraid of a meaningless life than of death. You can help your loved one to define who he is and what his life has meant. This is his search for meaning. Reminiscing helps him accept death and let go of the fear of death, and with that, we have reconciled a life lived with purpose and meaning. His fear or acceptance of death depends on whether he has found meaning in life. Help him to realize his significance and legacy by asking questions such as:

- What are you most proud of?
- What was your happiest day?
- What was your biggest challenge?
- What did you share with the world?
- What have you passed along that you learned?
- What has been important to you?
- How have you made a difference to even just one person?

Dying people report that the ultimate lesson is to love, and that in the end, only love matters. You can help your dying loved one know that the love she leaves behind is part of her legacy and will transcend her death. Discuss with her how she demonstrated love and how it will be remembered and valued in the future. To be able to understand and articulate the lessons of a lifetime—the truths about fear, anger, forgiveness, love, and joy—are the final gifts of peace. To accept and reconcile those truths means that she has come to terms with what has happened in her life and with what is happening now at the end of her life. This is spiritual work of meaning-making and integration that brings a sense of closure and peace so she can move on and let go.

When you help your loved one express his legacy in a life review, it is a way for him to continue his impact and to influence others in the future whether they are with us or not. Often our worst fear is that we will be forgotten. Help your loved one know how he will be remembered. Help him to avoid being remembered by default. Ask him how he wants to be remembered:

- How would you like to be remembered?
- How can we highlight your life and contributions?
- What title would you like on your obituary?

Find Your Caregiver Role

If you are fortunate to have more than one caregiver participating in your loved one's end-of-life needs and wishes, it is helpful to identify the skills and perspectives of care with which each person is most comfortable. Like members of a symphony, each participant can use her strengths and experience to create the most harmonious outcome. Ask each member what she is able and willing to do and choose roles so that caregivers coordinate and synchronize care, rather than deplete their limited resources of time and energy. In the best-case scenario, each of the roles is covered and caregivers work together, appreciating the strength and support they provide each other and your loved one. Examples of contributing roles you might step into are:

Medical Advocate
- Advocate based on your dying loved one's unique needs, agenda, and values.
- Advocate for clarity of communication; break down medical terms; repeat as often as necessary.
- Advocate for timely, honest prognosis of disease *if* the patient wants to know.

Accompany your loved one to appointments. Carry a tape recorder to record information. Patients and caregivers are often overwhelmed by new information and diagnoses, medical jargon, the emotions that follow, and processing decisions; it is understandable that everyone involved can easily forget important information. Recorded information can be reviewed later with the patient and family members, and transcribed for organization.

Empower your loved one to give voice to her wishes, concerns, and questions; help her be as active a participant in her care and decision making as she is comfortable with. Teach, model, and give her skills, language, and resources if necessary. Help the patient help herself to live her life independently and with dignity for as long as possible.

Understand, acknowledge, and advocate for your loved one's definition of family. Family to her might include non-blood relatives or pets that she needs to see and with whom she needs to finish business. Find a comfortable way to bring her pet onto the bed for a good-bye. If your dying loved one is spending time in an intensive care unit of a hospital, arrange for private time without audio or visual monitors to preserve the privacy and intimacy between partners.

Acknowledge and honor your loved one's intuition, insights, dreams, and visions. They too are part of the wisdom and lessons in dying. Dreams and visions can be some of the most reassuring and hopeful moments to the patient.

I am reminded of a friend, Donald, who was dying in the hospital, stomach cancer taking his life. His wife, Marilyn, called at the usual time that they checked in with each other. "I can't talk now, Marilyn. I have to get back to Alaska," he said. "It's so beautiful! I don't want to miss a minute. I'll fly back later, and you can call me then." Marilyn called him the next morning and did not refer to the incident as a dream or suggest that medication had altered his perception of reality. Instead, she mentally met him where he was, acknowledged his experience, and asked about his trip to Alaska, expressing interest in every detail of his itinerary. Together they laughed and talked about each place he was able to visit. She was as excited for him as he was that he had been able to visit the one place that his illness had precluded him from. Or had it?

Home Manager

You can help control the environment in spite of the lack of control over the disease or progression of decline. Create a gentle environment toward the end of life that reflects the loved one; be particularly attuned to distracting noises of television, electronics, and telephones. Inquire about your loved one's preferences in order to set up the environment that best reflects the person.

Companion or Personal Aide

The companion is that personal aide who may be the patient's groomer or who provides any level of emotional or physical support. The companion might be the person who is most comfortable with physical touch and best able to model its healing power. Merely placing a soft hand on his arm, gently stroking the side of a worried face before an x-ray, or drying his skin with a soft, fleece sheet after a bed bath can make all the difference in a patient's anxiety and sense of safety.

I've thought of myself as a midwife, providing emotional support and reassurance during this time of labor into the next life. I understand the journey of dying to be like the journey of delivering a child; the pain of dying can be similar to the pain of labor. This metaphor illustrates a physical pain born out of emotional loss and changes that happen when we move into a new stage of life. We can be frightened of the unknown or trusting of the journey that millions have taken before us. Both can be viewed as grotesque and painful, unless we understand the processes as normal, natural rhythms of life. Both are endings as well as beginnings, and once through the transition, any pain that was experienced is negated by the outcome—once pain, now accepted, is not held as suffering.

Researcher

The researcher provides research, information, statistics about the disease, treatment options, clinical trial updates, healthcare provider options, information about what to expect and how to prepare, and community resources. Information can be found through the internet, medical organizations and agencies, and libraries, and through personal contact with others. The researcher can create a binder to contain all medical information so it can be updated and retrieved easily by the patients and caregivers.

Facilitator

The facilitator asks the dying person what she would like to do with whatever time she has left. What would she like to see? Whom would she like to talk with, write to, or visit with? You can facilitate contact or communication via the phone, letter writing, or the internet, or in person. Acknowledge difficult requests, and try to find creative solutions. If you sense that your loved one is holding on, ask her directly, "Is there something you need to do before you die, and can I help in any way?"

During my father's dying, I opened the conversation this way: "Dad, no one knows how much time you have left, so let's hope for the best but plan for the worst. What do you want to do if you only have two weeks left?" He told me that he wanted to ride his horse one more time. I knew that was a difficult request because it would require that he leave the home and go against medical advice, and hospice would not sanction the activity while he was their patient. But it was important to him—following through would add to the quality of the life he had left. So I located a portable oxygen tank and took him out of the house. It would take three people to hold him up on his horse while he barely trotted along, but we were going to do everything within our power to see that his wishes were fulfilled. There is usually a way to get things done if we stay open to options.

As a facilitator, you might serve as the correspondent, writing letters for your loved one to family and friends whom he does not have the energy to speak with. You can help him to say what he needs to share in order to finish business, send off treasured items before rather than after his death so he has the joy of giving while he is alive. You might help your loved one designate people or organizations he wishes to remember after his death with gifts or memorabilia, mindful of existing wills.

You can be that link to the outside world that helps preserve relationships in spite of deteriorating health. You might be your loved one's personal assistant to help keep track of letters and to read cards that arrive for him, make telephone calls for him, help him remember family celebrations so he continues to be a part of important family rituals. Help your loved one stay involved and connected to the family fabric and events that are important to him.

Family Mediator

You might have the needed skills to be a family mediator, who brings family members together, begins conversations, follows up with family members, and makes sure everyone is informed, included, and consulted if that is the wish of the patient. You can help manage family expectations: "I am sorry, but Mom just does not have the energy right now to visit with you." You can answer questions about the illness or prognosis that she may not want to address or repeat: "The doctor believes Mom has between two and four weeks left." Set and maintain healthy boundaries: "Mom is withdrawing from her old routines, so she no longer wishes to visit with the neighbors." You can help keep family members focused on the big picture: "I understand that you want to call the ambulance, but we all agreed that we would follow Mom's wishes, and she told us that she wants to die at home."

The family mediator might be that authority that sets and maintains a moratorium on judgments and labels. The mediator models behavior and encourages everyone to be patient and compassionate, and to allow for differences during life's most trying of times. This role helps to remind caregivers that they all serve a mutual goal—to care for their loved one and carry out his or her wishes. And the mediator encourages each family member to participate in his or her own authentic good-bye rituals.

Listener

The listener is encouraging and becomes the role model for talking about what is difficult, the elephant in the room that most people are wasting valuable energy trying to avoid. Acknowledge difficult feelings. Allow for different expressions of anger, fear, resentment, frustration, guilt, confusion, and doubt; they are uncomfortable feelings, and every bit a part of the death, dying, and grieving experience. Feelings come in waves and surges, and they do not have to make sense.

Let people tell their story without judgment or comparison. Listen to their stories, careful not to interject stories of your own life. Validate their experiences, feelings, and point of view without diffusing the energy by interpreting, fixing, or offering advice unless you are asked.

Adapt to the dying person's wishes, from periods of silence, to reading, to massage, to prayer, to holding his hand. Stay fluid and flexible, valuing the healing power of silence. Listening in silence, with validation as the response, allows the dying person a safe place to explore confusing feelings. It gives him a container for his pain, confusion, and anger. There is a relationship balanced between sharing feelings openly and honestly, and maintaining emotional well-being and health. Sometimes the most helpful gift is to listen, not to answer. The greatest service is to be aware and present in each moment, with each breath. That silent, observant awareness is like a sacred chalice that holds the dying and his unique experience.

Even children can make a difference. Encourage their participation in age-appropriate tasks and sharing, such as selecting clothes or running errands. Children who participate can experience greater self-esteem and lower death anxiety as a result of their contribution. Depending on their age and ability, a child can read a favorite story or daily mail to the dying loved one. A child can be taught the skill of massage and can maintain physical contact with the dying. Children can companion and just be with their loved one, participating in simple, favorite activities such as watching a movie or sharing stories. Depending on the child's maturity, simple medical procedures, such as swabbing chapped lips or changing wound dressings, can be taught and delegated.

Hope Is Always Possible for . . .

- Symptom control, pain management, palliative care
- Resolving personal relationships
- Supporting a dignified death

What to Say That Matters

- "I cannot change the fact that you have diabetes, nor can I stop death from coming. But I can make a difference in how you go through this."
- "I will be here for you whenever you want and however I can be."
- "I may not be able to change what happens to you, but I think together we can change how it feels."
- "You are not alone."
- "I don't know how we will do this yet, but I know we will do it together."
- "I am here."
- "No matter how hard it gets, I will be here. And as alone as you may feel, I am going to be right here, as close as you want me."
- "Moment to moment, we'll do this together."
- "Tell me what you want; tell me what you need."
- "You're the boss; we'll carry out your wishes."

Ways to Serve

1. Control the environment in spite of a lack of control over the disease or its progression:
   - Tidy up the house or your loved one's room.
   - Provide fresh flowers or bring in healthy potted plants.
   - Bring in food, groceries, and prepared meals.
   - Manage laundry; provide clean sheets and towels more often than usual.

2. Create rituals as daily continuity of care:
   - Ritualize the way you wake your loved one, for example, with a song, a kiss, or a touch.
   - Create a feeling of pampering when it is time for a bath or to clean up.
   - Set aside a designated time or space to read the daily mail.
   - Make a routine of taking your loved one out into a special part of the garden each day, if she is physically able.

3. Work in daily or nightly rituals:
   - Massage: Touch is a profound way to communicate emotions; touch can demonstrate our connection, tenderness, and caring for our loved one. Touch reduces anxiety, alleviates stress, and heightens a patient's ability to work through pain. It also provides an opportunity for routine assessment of any physical changes and needs.
   - Sounds: Listen to his favorite soothing music, or read his favorite magazine or book aloud.
   - Review the day: "What was the high point? What was the low point? What do you want to focus on tomorrow?" Listen, learn, and focus on solutions.

4. Pay attention to sensory details:
   - Apply favorite scented lotions.
   - Play her current favorite music or music from the past to evoke memories.
   - Hang wind chimes outside her window.
   - Put up a bird feeder or plant a flower box that she can view from her bedroom window.

5. Celebrate family history:
   - Offer her favorite foods.
   - Continue past celebrations and family traditions.
   - Provide a link to her old self and old connections; food and meal time serve as an entry point into stories and meaning-making.

6. Let your loved one remember, repeat, review, and process:
   - Review scrapbooks together and listen to his stories.
   - Ask: "Dad, let's look through your scrapbooks; I'd like to hear some of your stories again. . . . Tell me about the highlight of this event. . . . What did this adventure mean to you?"
   - Give him your full attention and interest as he repeats the same story as many times as he needs to. During repetition, the dying person is coming to terms, understanding and finding meaning in order to finish business.
   - Watch family movies and videos together. Ask: "What does this mean to you? What do you remember about this time?"

7. Be a gatekeeper:
   - Manage visitors and phone calls: the ill are fragile, overwhelmed, and need help to simplify and organize the end of life.

8. Organize a medical care binder:
   - Include all medical information, such as prescriptions, phone numbers, dates of hospitalization, community resources, respite care, and important people to notify.

9. Provide for care of patient's children and family:
   - Relieve your loved one of concern and responsibility. Identify the needs of the family, and facilitate their participation in care as much as they choose and are able.

10. Practice purposeful silence:
    - Often silence means more, and makes more sense, than words do. Stillness and silence can be the most helpful and reassuring activity in the moment.

NOTES

1. U.S. Department of Health and Human Services, *Health, United States, 2006: With Chartbook on Trends in the Health of Americans* (Hyattsville, MD: National Center for Health Statistics, 2006).

3

DYING MAY BE PAINFUL;
DEATH IS NOT

When you were born, you cried and the world rejoiced. Live your life in a
manner so that when you die, the world cries and you rejoice.

NATIVE AMERICAN PROVERB

Sometimes I imagine I am a cultural anthropologist. Just as Margaret Mead, the renowned American anthropologist, went to Samoa eighty-five years ago to explore, observe, and record the experience of a new culture, so too have I gone to a foreign land, previously unexplored and unrecorded. The land is a different culture—different from the one I find familiar. This land is the "other side"—the land after life, or life after death.

My vehicle was a near-death experience, and the path was through the tunnel and into the light. Since Margaret Mead's study and observation of Samoan culture, many have made a similar trip to that paradise in the South Pacific and come back to share comparable observations and insights about what the journey meant to them. The journey is not important. Rather, the positive changes and the contributions she made as a result of the experience are of importance—are worth thinking about.

Near-death research studies and Gallup polls indicate that more than fifteen million adults in the United States report having gone to another land through their own near-death experience.[1] When we add children's near-death experiences, and the similar reports experienced worldwide, the numbers are much greater. The age, gender, or nationality of the person who died and lived to tell about it does not alter the experience. Their observations are remarkably similar in what was seen, what was learned about others and themselves, and what it meant. A century ago, people may have doubted that such a paradise as Samoa existed. Many questioned Margaret Mead's powers of observation and interpretation, until others made a similar journey to the same place and returned with corroborating information, observations, and interpretations.

I might have doubted a place where we are reunited with loved ones who have died before us and where those once old or ill are fully healed. I could have been cynical about a place where we feel no pain or anxiety, and we are able to view our body without attachment to anything physical. It would have been unimaginable to know that after death there is the greatest sense of peace, acceptance, and love. I witnessed and experienced this other place on "the other side of death" just as millions of others have reported, and I came back with a new perspective about life and death.

My Personal Near-Death Experience: A New Relationship with Death

I had a near-death experience. As a result of that experience, my understanding and relationship with death changed. My mother's death and my near-death experience led me to my work with the dying, and they have made all the difference in how I am able to be with those who are dying and grieving. Some have said that I am able to "lean into" death when others pull away.

In 1982, when I was twenty-nine years old, I sat in a dentist's chair for a routine dental procedure. I was administered nitrous oxide as an anesthetic. I had rarely taken medicine or any kind of anesthesia like this, and perhaps this lack of exposure made me sensitive. For whatever reason, an immediate allergic reaction caused me to stop breathing. What I remember is that suddenly I was up in the corner of the dentist's office, looking down at the dentist, who was frantic. I looked at my body, and my eyes had rolled back into my head. I felt a strong compassion for the dentist—more than the level of concern I felt for what was happening to my body.

As I looked at the person in the chair, I had only a detached sort of fondness for my body, as though that physical shell was like used clothing that I could take to a donation center. I knew, as I looked at myself, that I was dead, but I felt no fear or anxiety. I was peaceful. The next thing I was aware of was that I was moving toward a tunnel. As I entered the tunnel, my mother appeared, just as I remembered her when I was a child. She seemed to stand with her arms open, ready to catch me and embrace me in this transition. I knew without a doubt that it was my mother and that she was healed, made whole again. Even after all these years, I am still moved when I recall how radiant, whole, and healthy she looked. She was once again my beautiful, vibrant mother.

My mother and I communicated only two things to each other. The communication was wordless, telepathic. I said, "I miss you." She said to me, "I know." The tone and intensity of her voice said everything. Then I said, "I love you." Again she answered, as though the importance echoed through canyons, "I know." What we said was everything I needed to hear.

The way she said "I know" was the message within the message for me. What I knew in that moment was that she had always been with me, that she had known everything. Understanding that, there was no need to tell her the details of my life. In fact, the details were not important. I could let go of her then, confident that she had been and would always be with me. That I moved away from her still surprises me, because logically it would seem I would want to stay with her forever, but I felt myself pulled onward. There was a pinpoint of light off toward the end of the tunnel, and I knew I had to go to it.

There was no sense of time. The tunnel was very big, round, and encased in the color of robin's-egg blue and mother-of-pearl iridescence. I heard an ethereal sound that floated through the tunnel, but it was not any form of music I recognized. I came into the presence of a Light, which was in front of me at first. Then it expanded and came around my sides. It moved as though it was enveloping me like a soft, warm blanket. I realized I was not only inside the Light, but the Light and I were one. There was no separation, and we were made of the same essence. I was a drop of water returned to the ocean.

As I look back, I believe that there is not a word or a name that can capture the essence of the Light. The energy, or fabric, that surrounded me communicated compassion and unconditional love for every living thing. I suddenly had wisdom and a profound respect for the sacredness of all life, and I knew that there was not just one path by which to understand. This Spirit and loving presence that welcomed me home was larger, wiser, more compassionate and inclusive than any formal religion or word ascribed to it.

If someone wants to call it Buddha, or Jesus, or God, I would say yes. For me the closest descriptor is to call it Love. In its presence I knew that I was forgiven for anything and everything. I knew that I was loved unconditionally, and I knew that would never, ever change. The word *bliss* doesn't even come close to describing the experience. This "place" was home. I had arrived in a state of grace, for which I was always searching. I was loved, as I had always wanted to be loved. I never wanted to be any other place. I wanted to stay there forever.

In this state, I knew that death was an illusion and that we survive the demise of our body for a grander experience. I knew there was nothing to fear in death. I knew that my consciousness survived death. I knew, too, that there is no such thing as distance between loved ones. I realized that all my fear and grief had stemmed from an illusion of separation. This feeling of love, connection, and freedom was beyond what I ever dreamed possible.

So when I heard the Light communicate, "You have to go back," I yelled, "No!" from the center of my being. With compassion, the Light repeated, "You have work to do. You must go back." Once again I shouted, "No!" with all the force I could muster. It was then that I felt myself being pulled back through the tunnel in a churning, whirling sensation.

My next awareness was that I was back in the dentist's chair. I noticed how heavy and dense my body felt. The dentist was clearly upset, and I was oblivious to how he was assessing whether I was lucid and healthy. It was obvious to me that he wanted me out of his office. I left stunned and overwhelmed with a variety of emotions. I knew that what I had experienced was real, and I knew that I was not crazy. But I did not have words or context for this near-death experience, and I felt completely disoriented.

There was a long period afterward that I lived in confusion, alternating between feelings of sadness about my return to this so-called life and feelings of awe as I recalled the experience. I felt guilty that I had not wanted to return to this life with my loving husband and two-year-old daughter, the two people who meant more to me than anyone in this world. But I still cannot imagine voluntarily leaving the presence of that Love and Light.

I continue to have many moments of wanting to go "home." My comfort comes from knowing I am not separated or apart from that Love. I have an overwhelming appreciation for the opportunities and responsibility of being in this world. I know now that this is a world where we are given the opportunity and privilege to do our work, where we learn our lessons. So I attend to the work I am meant to be doing here—I care for those who are dying and grieving.

≻≍≺

Lessons from a Near-Death Experience

- Death is merely a transition to another dimension.
- The dying do not suffer at the moment of death.
- The deceased continue to exist in some other form and dimension.
- Consciousness continues after death.
- The deceased are healed and whole after death.
- Contact may occur between the deceased and the living.
- Loved ones are reunited in death.
- Each life has purpose and a plan.
- Practicing unconditional love is the most important work during our lifetime.

Aftereffects of a Near-Death Experience

The importance of the near-death experience lies in its meaning and its aftereffects. The scientific research and medical investigations of the fifteen million people in the United States who have reported near-death experiences help us to enlarge our understanding of death. Research out of the University of Connecticut, through the International Association for Near-Death Studies, and professional journals such as *Death Studies* corroborate the evidence and the lasting effects of the experience. With understanding comes a lessening of our fears. Those reports consistently reveal that during their dying, or at their death, these people sensed no pain, experienced no anxiety about being separated from their body, and felt no fear. These are firsthand reports of death from the inside, rather than the hypothetical expectations from those observing from the outside. Thousands of people who have experienced death give testimony that they felt no physical pain or distress at the moment of death. Witnesses to their death feared that the dying were experiencing anxiety, fear, or pain while suffocating or enduring injury. Instead, those who have had a close call with death report they experienced a sense of floating, peace, and euphoria.

The power of the near-death experience is lasting and life altering. The most significant outcomes are that the fear of death disappears, appreciation for the gift of life increases, spirituality is stronger, and compassion and unconditional love become guiding life principles.

The bereaved often search for answers to questions such as: What happened to my loved one after death? Will I ever see him again? Did my loved one know I was with her? Did my loved one suffer at the time of his death? How can her death make sense? The findings from those who have gone through a near-death experience are important to share with those who are in the process of dying, and with their survivors (see Appendix D: Notes and Current Research on Near-Death Experiences, page 227).

Knowing what *is* experienced changes what we fear *might* be experienced. If we are less fearful of death, we will better prepare for it. We will participate more fully and be more peaceful and accepting. We will talk about it and communicate with others more openly—we will feel less alone. When a loved one is dying, she will feel that she was more involved in her living right up to the moment of her death. She will feel that she was heard and accepted. We will have a greater capacity to be present with, rather than repulsed by, the deterioration of the body, knowing that on the other side the body is healed. We will be able to sit through the last moments of dying, no matter what the dying process looks like, knowing there is no pain at the moment of death. As caregivers and survivors, we can be more helpful to our loved one, knowing she will not feel or remember the experience of death as painful. Rather, death is a release; it is like taking off an old, tight shoe that no longer fits. We have outgrown the body like clothing that is now too restrictive; now the soul needs to run barefoot.

With modern medicine and the hospice philosophy, we can provide someone who is dying of a fatal illness with measures of comfort to relieve pain and suffering. A patient no longer has to feel that his symptoms cannot be addressed. When we are truly present with the personal, spiritual experience of the dying journey and not just the physical, medical aspects, the transition from living to dying can become as sacred, intimate, and profound as the process of being born into this world. Physical pain and symptoms can always be managed and contained with cooperation between doctor and patient. Suffering, hopelessness, and helplessness can be attended to and eased when we accept, validate, and understand the patient and his experience. All pain, whether physical, emotional, or spiritual, can be softened and transformed.

Do Not Judge Your Loved One's Experience of Death

Your perceptions and what you see of your loved one's last hours or minutes of living are not necessarily what the dying person experiences. The external responses do not represent the internal reactions. If, at the moment of death, the body reacts in a convulsing way, do not be deceived into believing that pain is the summation or the final experience of their life. If you hear a death rattle—the throat's constriction at the end of life—do not be misled by your fear that she is feeling suffocated or terrified. If you believe in the pain or decay of disease as the primary experience, you are more likely to be afraid and to limit your ability to be present and help.

The value of these thousands of similar near-death experiences is the common theme that death does not bring anxiety to those passing through it. At the moment of death, the person understands that the body was a vessel through which the soul experienced itself. He has no concern for his body, and there is no investment in the drama of dying. Dying is understood as merely a means of leaving the body, of finishing the work in this life. From a higher perspective, it is understood that one death is no more tragic than another. This is important to restate, for many misunderstand the nature of death and view it as a punishment or a curse. A sudden death stops body functioning; a sudden or unexpected death is no better or worse, tragic or heroic, than death from a long-term illness that is progressive or expected. The process of dying may be painful, but the moment of death is not. Death is not painful. There is peace. There is release. There is Light at the end of the tunnel.

This way of knowing death is important because it can deepen our ability to respond and to be present. We no longer turn away from the illusions and limitations of the body. When we understand the fuller context of dying, we no longer believe that our loved one is just a physical form. We see the dying process and the needs of the dying from a holistic perspective. Then we respond to not only the physical needs but also the invisible and often-ignored needs of the spiritual, emotional, and relational dimensions. We are able to help our dying loved one and ourselves to trust in our abilities to be present in the process without fear and to participate more fully. We do not hold memories of our loved one leaving his or her body; we ignore the struggle during illness and dying, remembering instead the gift of our time together, the ways we loved, and the life that was shared. In the end, only love is remembered. What survives of us is our love.

How to Respond to Your Dying Loved One's Pain

- Take time, before doing anything else, to pay attention and listen.
- Serve as a mirror for the person in pain: calm and center yourself so he can see what it looks like to feel calm and can mimic you.

- Use soothing, repetitious motions, sounds, and routines such as massage or vocalized breathing to calm a person and help her regain an inner sense of balance.

How to Say Good-Bye

The dying person often needs permission from loved ones to die. He needs to know that you feel he is not deserting loved ones and that the survivors will be able to go on without him. Especially as a parent, the dying person needs to know that he is not abandoning family and that his loved ones will be okay without him.

- "Dad, thank you for loving me all these years. You've taught me everything I need to know. I'll be okay. You can let go."
- "Mom, the whole family is here. We will all take care of each other. It's your turn to rest now. We will miss you, but we will never forget you."
- Grandpa says that for the last several days he has had visits from his deceased wife; he is happy and excited to see her again. "Grandpa, it's okay to go and be with Grandma. She is waiting for you. You can go whenever you want."
- "Kurt, it's all right to die. We will always love you. You have fought for so long; you have not let us down."

How to Be with a Loved One Who Is Not Responsive (Alzheimer's, Coma)

- Watch her heartbeat on the hospital monitor; breathe or stroke gently in the same rhythm with her heartbeat.
- Breathe with the same rhythm as his breath as a way to communicate "I am with you" without using intrusive words.
- Use touch as communication, as though you are softly talking to her. Gently stroke her arm in the same rhythm as her breath.
- Speak as if your loved one hears you. Patients who have returned from comas are often able to repeat verbatim what has been said to and around them while they were comatose.

How to Know When the Moment of Death Is Close and How to Respond without Fear

Arms and legs of the dying person may become cool to your touch; underside of the body may become darker in color.
RESPONSE: Cover your loved one's body with light, warm blankets.

The dying person sleeps more and is more difficult to arouse.
RESPONSE: Be present, still, and serene with him as he sleeps; spend time with him as he wishes while he is alert.

The dying person may become disoriented or confused about time, place, and people.

RESPONSE: Demonstrate patience; gently remind her of the day, time, and people if she asks.

There is an increase in oral secretions in the back of the throat, and the sound of a death rattle may be heard.
RESPONSE: Elevate the head with pillows; swab the mouth and lips with lemon-glycerin swabs for comfort measures.

The dying person may lose clarity of hearing or vision.
RESPONSE: Keep room or bedside lights on. Repeat what he cannot hear, but always assume the person can hear whatever you are saying—do not talk about him as though he were not in the room or could not hear you. Avoid background noise; turn down the volume of the television or music to decrease background noise before speaking.

The dying person may talk about or to deceased loved ones; she may report seeing things or people that we do not.
RESPONSE: Listen with interest. Validate her experience; if she has the interest and energy, help her talk about the meaning or message of the experience.

The dying person may pick at the bed sheets or clothing and appear restless.
RESPONSE: Soothe the agitation with gentle touch or stroking; speak calmly with reassurance so any confusion or anxiety is calmed.

The dying person has less interest in food and drink. Her appetite and capacity for intake lessens significantly.
RESPONSE: Provide food supplements if needed, but do not force food on the dying. This is a natural withdrawal of life interest, the body's way of conserving energy.

The person's breathing patterns change. You may notice longer spans of time between breaths, shallow breathing, or gasping that sounds like a fish out of water.

RESPONSE: Elevate the head of the bed or add pillows under the person's head to relieve irregular breathing. Calm the person by speaking and touching gently if he is agitated.

Urine output will decrease as death approaches.

RESPONSE: If the person has a catheter in place, a nurse or aide may irrigate the catheter to prevent blockage.

NOTES

1. Brendan I. Koerner and Joshua Rich, "Is There Life After Death?" *U.S. News & World Report* (March 23, 1997).

George Gallup and William Proctor, *Adventures in Immortality* (New York: McGraw-Hill, 1982).

4

DEATH IS NOT THE END

The truth is sort of mysterious and sometimes has nothing to do with facts.
OLIVER SACKS, NEUROLOGIST, PSYCHIATRIST,
AND AUTHOR OF *AWAKENINGS*

I am reminded of the hundreds of people I have sat with just before they took their last breath. For a while I volunteered as a lay chaplain in a county hospital. I visited patients and offered what I could—my attention and presence, a listening ear, a game of cards, or a gentle massage.

I returned to visit eighty-six-year-old Clara, who had been unconscious for several days; the doctors did not expect her to last through the night. On one side of her stood her eighty-eight-year-old sister Ann, and on the other side was eighty-four-year-old Esther. I stood at the foot of the bed speaking softly to Clara. Why, when she was unconscious? Because our sense of hearing is the last to go, and I have spoken with many coma patients who told me how comforting it was that I spoke *to* them as though they were conscious and functional rather than *about* them as though they were not in the room.

I told Clara that her sisters were there and that I had returned. I told her that she was being cared for and that there was nothing to fear. All of a sudden Clara opened her eyes and stared to the left of me with the softest smile.

"Joe, Joe!" she said.

"Who's Joe?" I asked Clara.

Her sisters, both shaking their heads, chimed in with "He's her husband, but he's been dead twenty years" and "It must be the stroke." The joy in Clara's eyes told another story. As she looked at the spot to the left of me, all traces of age, pain, and disability were gone. Her sister patted her as though she needed to be calmed. My response was "Clara, where else would Joe be at a time like this?" It is common at the end of life for the dying to claim that they see and hear a significant loved one such as a spouse or a parent.

We do not always recognize how many people we have made a difference for in our lives. Dying can be an opportunity to become aware of the many lives we have touched and to whom we have mattered. As your loved one is dying, he may become aware of a surprising number of deceased visitors, often many that fill the room to capacity at the end of life, who come in support and validation of a life well lived. These friends in spirit come to soothe and escort your loved one out of one room and into the next. I liken these old friends and loved ones to coaches encouraging the star player in the final game of his season, or to midwives who help during the birthing process. How might the dying person's fear be different, and your grief be lessened, if we approached death as a beginning rather than an end? We would be better able to let go if we knew loved ones and old friends accompanied them, and no one ever dies alone.

The message from the deceased is consistent and comforting: *I am here. You are not alone. Everything is all right. There is nothing to fear.* As we, who are alive, can offer assistance and be of service on this side, so too can deceased loved ones on the other side be of comfort and guidance. The awareness that no one dies alone is comforting to the bereaved, relieving them of anxiety, guilt, and fear. Why would we deprive our loved ones of that comfort? Why would we question their experience? How does it serve anyone to doubt that communication?

Instead, we could all feel comforted with the hope that we will be reunited with deceased loved ones, that no one is alone during this departure, that joy rather than fear and resistance will mark our transition, and that all is well. We must not allow anyone to minimize visionary experiences. When a loved one reports communication from someone who has gone before her, we need to listen with an open mind even if we might not believe this ourselves. We serve our dying loved ones when we can help them experience life with all its lessons and mysteries. We can validate and support them. We must make no judgments based on our own belief or disbelief.

It is important to know that no one dies alone. From thousands of Gallup reports and studies by prominent researchers in the field, such as Dr. Bruce Greyson, Dr. Kenneth Ring, and Raymond Moody, the near-death experience consistently is described as process of transition during which the dying are met by loved ones on the other side (see Appendix A). No one dies alone, though it may appear from our limited perspective that no one else was in the room at the time of death.

I have heard from many family members about their regret and guilt that they were not present for their loved one at the moment of death. Loved ones and caregivers may have spent months serving and comforting through an illness, but for one reason or another, they were not able to be with the dying person when he took his last breath. The family had the hope or expectation that being present at the moment of their loved one's death was what he wanted, and they feel guilty and remorseful for missing the moment of death. I have explained that if that had been so, the dying would have waited.

Is it not comforting to know that your dying loved one departed on his terms, in his timing, in his authentic way? Can you imagine how difficult it must be for a mother to hear her daughter beg her not to leave? How could she resist her child's needs yet know that life as she wanted it was over? To linger or hold on is to say no to loved ones who went before, whom she has longed to be reunited with.

Death's Timing Is a Mystery

More times than I can count, I have heard a doctor say, "He should be dead" or "A patient with this much internal damage doesn't usually make it," yet he lived on until all his family could be with him. I have been with many families who gather around a loved one in the hospital, hold vigil for days, and then finally go home for one hour to shower and change clothes. When it is during that time away that their loved one dies, I am not surprised. It is difficult for dying people to leave with so much love in the room, holding them here. We need to know that our loved ones die when they choose, from a deeper, soul level.

Each person dies in her own way, and in her own timing. We must not take her departure personally. It is not a condemnation of you that she died when you were not with her. Your loved one's choice was not to leave you; she is leaving a body that no longer serves her. She is moving on, in the right time, for her journey. It's better to see the timing of her death from her perspective, with acceptance, as perfect timing, and as a reflection of her love.

To know that a loved one chose the timing of his death when we were not present may be his last gift. If we can trust that his passage was gentle because there were no emotional obstacles or obligations holding him back, we can be more at peace. If we know that our loved one floated softly into the arms of many who had waited patiently to be reunited with him, wouldn't that bring us a measure of comfort? Could we trust that we will one day be met with the same outpouring of love?

How to Be Present at the Moment of Death

- Make no judgments; do not take her dying personally if she dies when you are not with her.

- Give the dying permission to go.
- Honor his wishes; use his values and ethics right up through the moment of death.
- Prayers, poems, and hymns may be comforting, depending on the person.
- Silence and a soft voice help maintain the sanctity of the process.
- Treat the time and the space as though they are holy; remove all distractions and drama.
- Provide gentle touch.
- Offer tenderness through all senses.
- Honor and validate visions, voices, and visits from deceased loved ones who have gone before.

After-Death Communication

After-death communication is a relatively new field of research that focuses on the spontaneous experiences of people who report contact by a deceased loved one. The communication includes sensing the presence of the deceased, feeling a unique touch, smelling a meaningful fragrance, seeing or hearing the deceased, or meeting the loved one in a dream or vision. This sense of presence, in any form, can happen immediately after death or months or years later.

This extraordinary phenomenon is actually very ordinary. From polls conducted by the National Opinion Research Center and reported in journals such as the *American Journal of Hospice Care, Death Studies,* and *OMEGA: Journal of Death and Dying,* researchers have made a conservative estimate that at least fifty million Americans, or 20 percent of the population, have had one or more experiences of after-death communication. More than two thirds of widows in America have had some form of contact with a dead person.[1]

After-death communication has been recorded throughout history as far back as 30 BC by the prominent Roman statesman Marcus Tullius Cicero, who wrote of contact by the deceased in his two-book treatise *On Divination*. The phenomenon was used for the central plot in William Shakespeare's *Hamlet* and Charles Dickens's *A Christmas Carol*. Christians of some denominations interpret the Bible to be full of instances of after-death communications from Jesus and multiple appearances by Mary. As more people share their experiences of ADC (after-death communication) and it becomes the norm rather than the exception, people will become aware and accepting of its healing potential for the dying and the bereaved. Whether you are religiously oriented, agnostic, scientific—or whatever tradition you honor—the research and reports of ADC help us shed our fears, so we can become more comfortable with death.

Acceptance of the phenomenon of ADC is important because it can relieve fear and anxiety for the dying and the bereaved. There is most often a sense of profound relief that we continue to be connected to our loved one. There is a sense of peace knowing that consciousness survives and our loved one continues to exist. When dreams of the deceased are reported, they are described as being more than a dream, and the effects have a profound impact on the intensity of their grief.

Often, dreams and the messages they carry are the turning point for adapting to a life without the deceased. The messages in dreams are personal and meaningful. Seeing the deceased as healthy, whole, and energetic gives the bereaved hope that there is healing after death. Healing happens even though physical survival does not. Such a vision can erase the torment of remembering a long, painful illness. A dream in which the deceased delivers a message—such as *I'm okay* or *I'll see you again*—leaves the bereaved with hope and reinforces a belief in life after death. Dreams and their messages can provide relief for unanswered questions.

The promise of reunion with the deceased loved one allows the bereaved to move on and live more fully in the present. The bereaved are able to develop and invest in a different form of relationship with their loved one. After-death communication is beneficial, healthy, and adaptive (see Appendix E: Notes and Current Research on After-Death Communication, page 237).

The Importance of After-Death Communication

- Encouraging the living to continue on with life
- Answering questions about the death
- Confirming that the bereaved continue to be loved
- Providing evidence that connection continues beyond death
- Defusing guilt
- Correcting false assumptions or information about death
- Providing an opportunity to finish emotional business
- Allowing an opportunity to say good-bye

No One Dies Alone; No One Grieves Alone

As the end of our loved one's life approaches, we begin to understand that there is no separation between loved ones, even after death. Those who pre-decease them comfort the dying; they serve as guides to the other side, reducing fear and anxiety. Your dying loved one leaves with love, literally, because he or she is escorted with love and by loved ones. When we have hearts that are free from fear, we can feel the love in the room as if we were in a sacred space, like a temple.

In the same way, those who are deceased comfort those who are grieving. As those who died before, now the deceased return with love and compassion to comfort those who are mourning. After-death communication can be experienced as an auditory contact (hearing the way he whistled), an intuitive sense (feeling the hair stand up on the back of your neck), an olfactory experience (smelling her favorite perfume), a physical sense of a presence in the room, or electrical signs or manifestations. Visions and dreams are contacts to confirm the reality of a continuing bond and relationship. Any of these experiences help those left behind come to terms with the change in the nature of the relationship, further helping them to trust the lasting connection. All forms of communication serve to reduce the anxiety of separation, soothe the pining for loved ones, and express that all is well.

On the first anniversary of my father's death, I felt alone and sad, and I wished for the comfort of his physical presence, even as I believed in our continuing connection. So I talked out loud to him, saying, "I feel so alone." Immediately from down in the basement, the stereo came on at high volume with "Hawaiian Soul," the song that I had sung softly to him as he died in my arms. I rushed downstairs, thinking maybe a car had gone by or a plane had flown overhead that might have caused an electrical surge that turned on the stereo. Then I paused, felt his presence in the room, and laughed. Of course he would be there to comfort me. And knowing about after-death communication means that no one has to grieve alone.

The ongoing connections of love serve to remind us of mysteries—beyond understanding and nevertheless true. Our connection with our loved one reminds us of what is essential. We revive the person we conjure up and evoke the feelings that define our relationship. When we recall, we are recognizing, once again, the truth of our connection. We are mindful of the invisible bond that is not destroyed by death.

It is important to acknowledge the ways that our loved one continues to be a part of our life, and to validate the importance and meaning of the moments when they happen. As with death, it is time that we normalize the pre-death visions and the after-death communications for what they are and accept the positive impact they have upon our living.

We are not alone. We do not live alone, even when we feel lonely. We do not die alone, even when we feel afraid. We do not grieve alone, even when we feel isolated and misunderstood. We are not alone, but we often do not perceive this truth, so our fear and grief are an unnecessary burden. Fear and illusion diminish our great potential to give of ourselves during life and to receive comfort as we die. No one has to die alone or feel alone once we understand that there is a spiritual dimension caring for us during our dying and our grieving.

NOTES

1. Alice J. Longman, RN, EdD; Bonnie Lindstrom, RN, MEd; and Michele Clark, RN, MS, "Sensory-Perceptual Experiences of Bereaved Individuals," *The American Journal of Hospice Care* (July/August 1988), 42–45.

Kenneth Ring, "Near-Death Studies: An Overview," *Journal of Near-Death Studies* (Fall 1993), 10.

Bruce Greyson, MD, "Near-Death Experiences," in *Varieties of Anomalous Experience: Examining the Scientific Evidence*, Etzel Cardena, Steven J. Lynn, and Stanley Krippner, eds. (Washington, DC: American Psychological Association, 2000), 315–52.

5

WE CAN COPE

There isn't anything that happens that can't teach us something. One can't undo what's been done, but one can use it creatively. . . . The only thing is to accept, and let the scar heal. Scar tissue is the strongest tissue in the body. . . . I shouldn't be surprised if it's the strongest part of the soul.

MADELEINE L'ENGLE, *A HOUSE LIKE A LOTUS*

If we believe we cannot cope with our loved one's dying, we move away and do not become a participant in service. Are we unable or unwilling? If we can identify that we are not able to help, it may be because we do not have the information with which to act, have not been taught the skills, or do not have the confidence that comes from experience and practice. If we can identify that we are unwilling, it may mean that despite having the information, skills, and ability, we have a resistance against participating.

We can learn to live with dying so that we can live without fear. If we adopt different perspectives, we will be in the world with more resilient attitudes, and we will make different choices about supporting our loved one during dying, as well as our choices about our own death. Perhaps the most important choice we can make is to live without fear and to die without fear. When our fear of death is healed, we approach dying as part of a journey of self-determination that reflects our loved one's authentic self. When we allow our loved one to make choices freely, we can witness him being more in charge of his life, right up to the moment of his death. We experience him as a cocreator with a higher power rather than as a victim. The dying journey becomes an extension of life, reflecting our loved one's values and character.

Knowing That We Can Cope Matters

We are a society unskilled at feeling pain in appropriate and healthy ways without self-medicating or distracting ourselves from the challenges in the present. If we knew that we were able to cope, we would be more likely to be present, aware, and more available to be of service in a time of need. When we are able to cope, we focus outward and care for others because we know that our needs are met. We can be other-focused.

All of our fears, resistance, and anger are really a fear of death. When the fear of death is healed, we begin to fully live. We do not back away from what we came to do in this life and in the life of our loved one. We can accept the end of her physical life without giving up or giving in.

Fear is less psychological than it is about our attitudes. None of us comes into this world born with attitudes; we are taught how to view the world around us and how to feel about it. When we educate ourselves about our fear, we can change our attitudes to accept that fear is a common fact of life, and that others share similar insecurities. However we tell our story, the common denominator is that our fear keeps us from participating in the life we want to live. Fear is a voice within that says, "I cannot handle this!" How do you know that is true? How would you live your life and, specifically, care for your dying loved one, if you could let go of that fear? What would you do if you could act as if you could cope with the challenge? You would act and respond with as much as you know, and with the resources available to you in the moment.

The antidote to fear is the opposite voice that says with conviction, "No matter what happens, I can handle it." Diminishing fear comes

from the action of doing what it is we fear. Our response comes before
we feel better about the fear and ourselves. The fear may continue to be
there, but by confronting it and acting, we can transform our helplessness or paralysis into personal power and responsibility.

Often our fear is linked to negative self-talk that we might make a
mistake. We are afraid that a mistake will deprive us or our loved one
of something, and our need to control the outcome imprisons us, as
there is no one way or perfect solution. The status quo is not preferable
to participating with our best intentions, even with limited skills. But
when we shift our perspective and remember our values of caring and
sharing love, we cannot make a mistake. We are on a journey together,
experiencing love moment-to-moment, and grateful for the opportunities that arise through this unique challenge. The journey reveals
opportunities to love and to trust ourselves, despite the outcome. We
do not enter into the relationship with the expectation or the need to
control a specific outcome because the participation in the journey is
the reward.

A softer death comes from accepting reality rather than judging the
experience. The inner voice of judgment connects words to experience
through comparison and criticism. We know we are judging when we
feel our hearts respond with anger, fear, or tension.

Your loved one's death will happen at some time. None of us will
stop that reality of the inevitable end to the physical body. But we can
change our loved one's experience by bringing our awareness to what
we do have control over. By changing our focus, we can cope from a
posture of equanimity that comes from *how* we live in each moment,
how we respond, *how* we care, and *how* we contribute. Knowing we can
cope is important because then we feel empowered, and we are more
likely to accept the opportunity to serve. Coping is the attitude we
need—along with information and skills—in order to make a difference. The following are ways you can identify when and how you are
coping so you can more confidently step into the role of service.

Coping Is an Attitude

Coping is an attitude of acceptance. We can choose to enter into the experience and feel it, to participate in it and to interact with others from the heart, rather than struggle to understand and experience it from the head. We can choose to accept what *is* instead of judging from our fears and needs. Coping is an attitude of inviting the present and what is right in front of us. Coping is an attitude of loving what is.

Imagine how different our experience might be if, instead of reacting with the fear that says, "I can't do this" or the judgment "I don't like this," we approached this challenge with the statement "This is an opportunity to love." Coping then becomes an opportunity to focus on the blessings within the circumstances. We look for the gifts rather than the burden. We experience what we have rather than what is being taken away or is lost.

Death and loss are not obstacles to happiness; often they are the very catalyst to opening one's heart and enriching life. An indication of good mental health is the ability to find the positive in any situation, an acceptance of challenges and blessings. Being mentally healthy and being able to cope means being able to find balance and awareness of the big picture.

Cancer may be a progressive, fatal disease that eventually takes a life, but an attitude of fatalism is an immediate death sentence. The defeatist chooses a state of mind that stops hope, drains the life energy, and obscures the beauty and blessings that make living with challenges worthwhile. When we find ourselves or our loved ones in a crisis of health, unable to control the inevitable outcome, we can control our mind and choose our attitude. In that choice, we have ultimate power. It is a discipline to pay attention to the present moment and actively look for the sacred in each minute, hour, and day. Our goal is to feel peace despite the outer struggle. Fears and attitudes are what impede peace, not illness. We can let them go.

Coping Is a Decision

With my father, I decided to bear witness to his living and his dying. I decided to transcend my fears and put aside my personal needs in order to make his life, right up through the end, my focus and my priority. I decided this and said to myself, *I can and will handle whatever comes.*

At the time of my mother's death, I could only feel that it was about loss and deprivation rather than the opportunity to serve and love her. Years later, I have come to understand her death differently. I decided to find the positive lessons and to make meaning from her death. Initially, I had to make sense of loss and discover the purpose in order to cope, in order to go on. Then I decided to search for something other than the tragedy. Mine was a decision of necessity— I needed to thrive rather than just survive—and that decision has made all the difference in my life. I searched for and found the perspective that would reflect that my mother's death was not a tragedy. By reviewing the experience and facing my fears and my pain, I rewrote my story. I uncovered the gifts and the growth that her dying afforded me. I changed the experience from tragedy to merely loss, becoming the author of my point of view.

This life is our opportunity to create. We are the travelers who can decide which path to take. We are artists displaying what we see, musicians interpreting what we hear, writers communicating what we feel. All that we experience is a choice of creation. It is the same for our death. We are the only ones who should be able to create and choose which path to take toward the end of our own life. Our death, in this way, is also our art. To the extent that we can make choices, our death is our *responsibility* to reflect our values and beliefs.

We can cope during the journey of a loved one's dying by making a conscious decision to be present, to stay open, and to participate in whatever comes during the process. We make that decision daily and bring ourselves back into an active state of discovery with the dying person and with the dying process. When we review the long list of daily chores, we see the tally as the openings to touch, listen, soothe, and support our loved one. We decide to stay in the moment, however it unfolds. We make the decision that this time is about active loving rather than suffering. We empower ourselves rather than sit in a blaming, victim posture.

We can cope and be much more helpful when we decide not to take death personally. We acknowledge that death is happening to our loved one, and we feel a myriad of personal reactions to the loss, but we remind ourselves that her death is not a reflection of who we are or who she is, nor is it judgment or punishment. Death happens to everyone, and neither our loved one nor we are singled out. We are a part of the human family sharing loss, pain, and the opportunity to care.

We want to make a conscious decision about how and where to participate in the dying journey. What are we able to do with the skills and experience that we have right now? What are we willing to do? What are we willing to learn, and how are we willing to stretch beyond our comfort levels for the sake of our loved one?

Coping Is an Action

Elie Wiesel notes "there is *response* in responsibility." *Respond* is a verb, and it is experienced as action when we lean into the challenge rather than move away because of our fears or feelings of inadequacy.

Coping is the process of managing the changing demands of a stressful situation. Coping is not an outcome. We do not cope once and for all. We manage by working through the process step by step, task by task, and day by day. Sometimes coping happens minute by minute, and we need to know that is enough.

We can break down coping tasks into concrete actions that move us toward our loved one and the needs that the situation presents. We can

define the meaning for ourselves in the work of caring by asking these
kinds of questions:

- Why am I helping?
- How am I demonstrating my values?
- What does this mean to me, about me, and about my loved one?

When we respond to the emerging needs of our dying loved one
with *I can handle this* rather than the disempowering fear of *What if I do
it wrong?* we develop a core strength and sense of security. Peace comes
from being able to handle challenges.

The taxing demands of the needs of our dying loved one, or the
work in grief, exceed the normal person's resources. The effort that it
requires to manage the demands and needs during this challenging
journey goes beyond the normal scope of experience, skills, and emotional capacity of most people. It is helpful to focus on coping as the
ongoing response to managing a crisis, rather than attempting to
achieve mastery over it.

Coping Happens in the Present Moment

As caregivers, we have fears and fantasies of what might happen in the
next moment, in the future. But in the present moment, we can see that
we are managing whatever challenges arise, even if we feel uncertain
about our skills. In the present moment, we are getting through and
addressing the needs of the dying. We can accept that we are coping,
managing, and handling the difficulties even while we are having overwhelming feelings of sadness, confusion, or frustration. We cope by
staying present.

While my father was gasping for air, I had to cope with feelings of
anxiety and sadness. I did this by staying present with him and mas-
saging his back to calm him. In the moment, I managed my feelings

and I stayed the course. Coping says, "In this moment, I can handle whatever arises, and in the next moment, I will manage with whatever resources I have."

Coping Happens Before, During, and After Death

As grief is experienced before, during, and after the dying process, so too is coping experienced during the entire process. It is helpful if, along the way, we can recognize our coping competency and can gain confidence to apply it to the next phase. The skills and coping perspectives we garner before a death may be applied after death. When we remind ourselves, "I have evidence that I handled this," during our loved one's dying, we can apply that same evidence as we cope during our grief after he dies. "I can handle this" encourages the acceptance of experiencing the reality of death, feeling grief, learning to live in a world without our loved one, and finding the meaning in the journey. We give ourselves permission to take whatever time we need to accommodate and live with the change in our lives.

Coping Is an Art

The many different ways that we cope with the circumstances of our loved one's active dying, his death, and our grief are expressions of who we are and what we believe. The ways that we express are art in themselves, and this art is happening every moment.

Because it is *our* art, and an expression of our love, it is a perfect communication and demonstration of who we are and what we care about. It is our connection to our loved one, our connection to ourselves, and our connection to a power greater than ourselves. There is no other way we *should* be in this journey, just as there is no other way our loved one *should* be other than who she is. We are both doing the best we can, with the resources and experience we have, in this moment.

Coping Is a Choice

We can experience the reality of our loved one's illness and his dying any way we choose. If we change our perceptions and understandings about death, the drama softens and the fear dissipates. We can choose how we see and make meaning of their dying and death. We can choose how we respond and how fully we will participate.

Coping Is Instinctual and an Act of Survival

Even when we do not know how to cope or we believe that we are coping well, we are striving for survival. We cope when we adjust to a new environment without our loved one. Coping is evident when we even attempt, without success, to offer a new skill or to consider a new perspective. We cope when we take over responsibilities that our deceased loved one always managed. Even in our failed attempts, we are adjusting, learning, and accommodating the new reality of being in a world with a dying loved one or in a life without her. We return, over and over, to the tasks at hand, and we learn to live in a new way, even while our attempts may be clumsy or poorly refined.

Coping Is a Way of Seeing Ourselves
and the World

Coping, like grief, is not a disorder or a disability. It does not make us half a person or less than ourselves. The feelings of grief do not need to be fixed. The griever does not need to be different. When we view our grieving self as normal, like everyone else who has loved and had to say good-bye, we are coping. When we accept what is, we are coping. We are able to see ourselves as normal people in a normal world during a normal phase of life. The end of life is to be expected. Feeling bereaved at the end of a loved one's life is a normal part of the journey.

We cope when we use our unique learning style to address our own needs. If you are a visual and tactile learner, you may use a metaphor to remind yourself that you are coping. The metaphor of a bag of stones seems a helpful way to remind yourself, *I can handle the grief.* When we see our grieving selves as a rough stone in a bag of polished stones, we are able to recall the gifts and blessings of our life. We are able to remember that our grief does not define our entire life, or the whole bag of stones. Perhaps, I think, the one rough stone is what has smoothed the other stones—and over time, the polished stones will shape and smooth the rough one.

Coping Is a Process

The challenges and responses of coping change as the demands of dying and grieving change. *Coping* is a present-tense verb. Each day is spent actively taking a step toward deeper understanding and acceptance of what is. It is movement toward meaning. Coping is a way of living with oneself and with the changes of your loved one. Coping is not giving up; it is not giving in; coping is not denying the pain or putting on an inauthentic face.

Coping is active. Coping addresses what we can do even as we accept that there are things we are not yet prepared to do. Coping is the ability to hold the pain and the gain at the same time. It is the willingness to use the word *and* instead of *but*: "I am heartbroken, *and* I must take care of the children" has a different power than "I am heartbroken, *but* I have to take care of the children." One position is empowering, and the other is crippling.

Coping means moving toward a *value,* rather than an *outcome.* You can decide that your goal is to care for the physical needs of your loved one. You can decide to play to strengths and contribute from your area of expertise or comfort, sharing the many other opportunities with other family and friends. Decide what your personal contribution will be and act upon that offering. There are many ways that you can contribute, make a difference, and be of service. It helps to be able to know your personal strengths, preferences, and style so you can enhance the support network for your loved one.

Here are many ways in which you can contribute and make a difference while you cope with the dying process:

Contribute by Staying Informed

Coping includes collecting information and knowing what may come next. Read and ask questions about the illness and death. Later on in this chapter you'll find more information about the signs and symptoms of approaching death—a sort of timeline of symptoms or "A General Roadmap toward Death," borrowed from the National Hospice and Palliative Care Organization (formerly the National Hospice Organization). Information and different points of view provide us with choices, options, and alternatives that feel empowering.

Say: What can you tell me that I have not considered? What are some options and choices that will add to the quality of his life right up to the end?

Make a Difference by Preparing ahead of the Expected Death

Sources of support are available through education, research, others' experiences and stories, skill building, rehearsal, mentoring, visualization, verbalizing, finishing business, and rituals.

Say: I do not know what is ahead, but I can learn and plan for contingencies. I can put resources and a system in place that anticipates her needs.

Contribute by Accepting the Reality of the Situation

When you see what is happening, rather than turn away, you honor your strengths and respond to the truth that you can do your best.

Say: I feel sad when I see you in pain, and I know we can find a way to ease your suffering.

Make a Difference by Building a Support Network

Coping says "I can ask . . ." for help, for respite and time off, for validation and feedback, and for self-care.

Say: I will find a support group for caregivers who are also caring for a dying loved one, where I can tell my story, feel understood, and not feel judged.

Contribute by Expressing Feelings

Find your feelings by expressing your thoughts. Thoughts lead to and create your feelings. Your feelings will inform you of your needs.

Say: Anything that is mentionable is manageable.

Make a Difference by Taking Care of Yourself

The easiest place to start with good self-care is with our physical needs; make sure you eat well and sleep enough. There is a reason why flight attendants ask you to put your own oxygen mask on before helping the person beside you in the event that the cabin loses air pressure. You need to care for yourself so you have the energy and sense of presence to be helpful to others. If necessary, ask someone else to do one of your tasks so you can attend to your own needs. Take care of your whole self, meaning the mind, body, and spirit.

When you take care of your mind, you might set limits on the amount of interference from television or radio, choosing instead to sit silently in a forest. You can take care of your body as animals do after stress, by finding a way to shake off and diffuse built-up trauma, sadness, or conflict. You might attend to your spirit by taking just thirty seconds to gaze out a window, tune out the stress, and meditate on gratitude.

Say: I need to delegate the chore of picking up medications so that I can recharge myself by walking the beach in silence.

Contribute by Finding the Blessing and Gift in Each Day

Make it your job to find the rainbow in the rain of each day. You can act as if you are blessed, even in the midst of chaos, confusion, and pain. Treat your loved one as someone who is *living with* illness rather than *dying from* illness. This is the most fundamental focus of peace work . . . to be the peace that you seek outside.

Say: I have not slept more than an hour tonight because I am hypervigilant to Dad's groans, moans, coughing fits, and attempts to get to the bathroom. I am up with him trying to intervene and make it easier. I put him to bed and find myself just watching over him. He breathes and is calm. Each inhalation seems like enough. I accept this as a gift, and I ask nothing more in this moment. He is here. I am here. We are in relationship.

How to Know When You Are Coping

- You can laugh and cry at the same story and not feel guilty.
- You do not take your loved one's death as a personal failure.
- You are able to list some good that happened in the midst of the sad.
- You can feel a sense of confidence, pride, and satisfaction in assisting in one of life's greatest challenges and toughest demands.
- You can support your loved one's environment so she can maintain some control and make authentic decisions about her death.
- You can create or maintain rituals that are meaningful.
- You have the capacity to shed inappropriate self-blame and guilt over what you did or could not do.

- You begin the work of self-forgiveness and address unfinished business.
- You can express your full range of feelings—feelings that are taboo as well as those that are condoned.
- You allow the dying person his own pace, his own terms, his needs, his meaning. You develop a compassion and friendship with the process of dying.

Make a Difference by Finding a Way to Accept Death

You can see death as an opening rather than a closing, a beginning rather than an ending, a graduation rather than an expulsion. You cope when you change your perception about death: choose to see death as something beyond bad, failure, or punishment. You cope when you understand death to be a natural progression and evolution. When you can assist another to die gracefully and gratefully, you have the comfort of knowing that she found peace before her death, rather than after it.

Say: I can surrender to the river of life with trust that it will carry my loved one and me where we are meant to be. I choose to see this death as a vehicle to another way of being for my loved one. I will focus on the privilege I have been allowed, to serve and love. In the worst of circumstances, we both have shared the thing that matters most.

Contribute by Not Taking Death Personally

You can cope when you are not angry at death. You can cope when you do not see your dying loved one or yourself as a victim. The transition of death happens to everyone and is an inevitable part of life, to all ages, in all cultures, in as many different ways as there are people.

Say: I can accept his death and do not have to protect myself by judging it. His death is his journey, in his time; this is not my time or my journey to make. I can focus and give his death my full attention.

What Coping Might Sound Like

- "I can feel my grief."
- "It's okay to grieve."
- "It's okay to ask for help."
- "I can cope with the pain."
- "In this moment I'm okay"... and in the next moment, "I'm okay"... moment to moment, "I'm okay, and I can handle this."

Make a Difference by Connecting to a Caring Community That Validates Your Feelings

It is the separation from loved ones and the shattering of human connections that most traumatizes us. What people need most during crisis is a healthy community that cushions the distress and suffering of loss. You heal in a community that provides consistent, patient, nonjudgmental care and facilitates acceptance of the death with rituals that express meaning about the person and the loss.

Say: I am strong enough to be vulnerable and ask for and receive support, as I have allowed my dying loved one to ask for and receive my support. I can trust others to truly listen and honor my feelings. I can trust that others will stay with me in my times of need.

We Cope Better with Information

We cope when we have information and knowledge about the dying process. With information, we can apply skills and be present to the needs of our loved one. The following is a timeline of symptoms and signs through the dying process.

One to Three Months before Death

- Withdrawal from the world and people
- Decreased food intake
- Increase in sleep
- Going inside of self
- Less communication

One to Two Weeks

The emotional-spiritual-mental state shifts to let go from the body, its environment, and all attachments.

Mental State
- Disorientation
- Agitation and restlessness
- Vision-like experiences
- Confusion
- Picking at clothes

Signs that the mind and body are preparing for the final weeks of life include a series of physical changes that are the normal, natural way in which the body prepares itself to stop. The appropriate responses are aimed at comfort-care.

Physical Condition
- Decreased blood pressure
- Pulse increase or decrease
- Complexion color changes (pale, bluish)
- Increased perspiration
- Respiration irregularities
- Congestion
- Sleeping but responding
- Complaints of body feeling tired and heavy
- Not eating, taking little fluids
- Body temperature hot or cold

Days or Hours

- Intensification of signs and symptoms that last one to two weeks
- Surge of energy
- Decrease in blood pressure
- Eyes glassy, tearing, half-open
- Irregular breathing
- Restlessness or no activity
- Purplish, blotchy knees, feet, and hands
- Pulse weak and hard to find
- Decreased urine output
- May wet or stool the bed

Minutes

- Fish-out-of-water breathing
- Cannot be awakened

PART II

MAKING A DIFFERENCE THROUGH BEREAVEMENT

6

GRIEVING IS A PROCESS

*Grief is like the wake behind a boat. It starts out as a huge wave that
follows close behind you and is big enough to swamp and drown you if you
suddenly stop moving forward. But if you do keep moving, the big wake
will eventually dissipate. And after a long enough time, the waters of your
life get calm again, and that is when the memories of those who have left
begin to shine as bright and as enduring as the stars above.*

JIMMY BUFFETT, *A SALTY PIECE OF LAND*

Grieving is an active coping process. Coping is a positive, life-affirming reaction that requires that we respond actively and invest energy. We cope when we investigate who we are without this person in the world. We cope through actively discovering and learning to be in the world without our loved one. We adjust and manage our grief by coming to a new understanding of our relationship and bond with the deceased. In these ways, as a coping mechanism, our grief has a purpose.

Grieving Happens Before, During, and After Death

Grief happens to some degree throughout a lifetime, because we are continually encountering loss. We feel grief when we lose our first love, whether that is a beloved pet or a first crush. We mourn our childhood friends and the dreams of growing up together when we move and lose our original neighborhood. Grief may strip us of our self-esteem when we lose a championship, or it might rob us of financial gain when we are fired from a job for which we have sacrificed.

When we are suddenly struck with the news of a potentially fatal disease, most respond with shock and denial so that the body and the mind can cope with the overwhelming news gradually, in a way that does not shut down or override any system. When we come to and the sting of reality begins to surface, we begin to grieve. When we are faced with our own death, we are afraid of the opportunities we will lose, the time that will be taken from us, and the people we will miss. We grieve even before we begin the obvious decline toward the end. Our imagination is heightened, in a protective and defensive mode, so that we can anticipate and not be taken by surprise. We might fantasize the worst so as to rehearse and practice getting through the scenes in a way that increases our confidence and proves to ourselves that we can cope. We exercise new emotional, physical, and spiritual muscles when we practice future possibilities; it is as though we are strengthening muscles we have not yet used.

In the midst of our loved one's dying process, as we observe the body's decline and participate in caring for him, we grieve the past. We grieve for what has been before; we react to the changes in his healthy body, his active life, and his participation in our lives. We also feel the loss of the essential spirit of our loved one as we watch the illness withdraw energy, as though water is draining from a bathtub. The core resources of our loved one are diminishing before our eyes, despite medical intervention.

All that is lost, and what or whom we feel deprived of, is not always lost in one moment. There can be a sequence of losses over a lifetime as a result of the death. There can be developmental losses or new realizations of what is missing as time passes and as we reach new milestones without our loved one. We grieve anew and with a different clarity as time goes on and new needs arise. A teenage boy whose father died when he was fourteen years old will grieve for the needs that are not met at that age, and when he becomes a new father, he will grieve differently for the mentor he needs and misses.

Grief Is Loss

Loss of trust   Loss of dreams
Loss of security   Loss of identity
Loss of faith   Loss of purpose
Loss of opportunity

Grieving May Include Denial

Denial is a protective, adaptive response to an experience that is perceived as threatening. It is a form of coping when we are unable or unwilling to accept some aspect of reality that would be apparent to others. Friends may accept the loved one's diagnosis of lung cancer and see the patient's physical decline, but the patient's son may not be able to repeat what he has been told, and he does not see or acknowledge that his parent cannot walk from one end of the room to the other.

Denial is not an all-or-nothing perspective. It might pertain to most aspects of the disease or only to certain parts. Denial can wax and wane with time; it might disappear or be relentless over the entire course of the illness until death. The fluctuating process of denial is unique to each individual and, like the process of healing through grief, it has its own timeline of resolution.

Denial protects us from feeling overwhelming anxiety about the painful external reality or our internal experience. We can move on from the stage of denial, but it is important to first honor denial and understand its value. Everyone has a right to his or her denial because it is a useful coping mechanism. Denial buffers the onslaught of overwhelming information, emotions, and change. Being in denial allows us the time to move from a simplistic view of the situation to finding ways to confront and deal with the challenges. The time out in denial can be viewed as a time in to form and affirm our own commitments and participation. Denial may appear to be shutting down, but time spent in denial and the process of coming to terms with the truth may actually keep us open to the reality of the illness and the dying journey.

Denial Is Working against You When . . .

- You feel unable to move forward in your life.
- There is unusual conflict within yourself, between you and your family, or between you and your friends.
- You are unable to make decisions even when you know you want to or need to.
- You numb yourself to feeling either joy or sadness through compulsive activity and distraction.
- You use drugs and/or excessive alcohol to block the reality of the death, and your feelings about it.

Grieving Is Hard Work

We do not get over grief. We work it. As Elizabeth Berg wrote in her novel *The Year of Pleasures,* "Healing hurts. . . . But hurting heals." We adjust to it. We learn from it. We incorporate the reality of death into our lives. We arrive at an understanding and create meaning about the death. We develop a deeper life because of it. We can abide with our loss peacefully instead of struggling against it.

Grieving Is a Physical Journey

Grief is biological and physical. It is communicated at a cellular level and is stored and remembered in the body, even if the mind is not conscious of its presence. Our grief can be triggered by a touch. My father always walked with me holding my elbow; whenever anyone touches my elbow like he did, my grief immediately arises and is tangible once again. Grief is rekindled through the sense of smell even when we are not conscious of it. I've felt tears run down my cheeks before I was even aware that I had just passed someone who wore my mother's favorite perfume.

Grieving Is a Physical, Emotional, Cognitive, and Spiritual Labor

Grief work is the cognitive and emotional process of coming to terms with a loss by confronting the reality of death and reorganizing our thoughts about the deceased, the events surrounding the death, and the world we live in without the deceased. Grief work is tedious, repetitive, difficult work and demands enormous energy. We often feel depleted when we grieve. Grief work is often spread out over months or years because a mourner does not have the physical, emotional, or cognitive energy to process it continuously or compactly. It is the body and mind's wisdom that processes grief and works through it gradually over time.

Grieving Has Its Own Timing

Grief comes in waves rather than as a steady rising tide. It is not a smooth-riding elevator, traveling a linear path from floor to floor. Grief changes as we work through our grief and participate actively in the tasks of grief. Time does not heal grief; it is how we use time that heals our grief. The reward of the work of grief is the acceptance of death and the skills to live in a world without our loved one. There is no end point to grief, but we can recognize when grief has transformed.

During my grief work after my father's death, I observed changes in my reactions and response to my father's physical absence from my life. I welled up and ached for him in the first year after his death. Now eight years later, I smile and am filled with a tangible sense of gratitude and joy when I think of him, even of his death. My investment in my grief work has meant that I spent time accepting the reality of his death; I learned ways to live without him and be happy; I discovered meaning in his death and gifts from my participation with that journey; I found ways to continue a relationship with him. All of this came through the time I spent alone in reflection with my feelings, and time passed with supportive loved ones validating my loss.

Renewed grief, or grief bursts, can come in waves and surges, and at unpredictable times. Any secondary, adjacent, or sudden loss creates a grief burst that requires an additional adjustment. Additional, subsequent losses exaggerate and compound our sense of being alone and left behind. Loss of a job, a home, a marriage, mobility or health, a pet, or a dream all remind us that we are vulnerable and suffer cumulative losses and deaths in many forms.

Each secondary loss requires its own set of grief reactions, from disbelief and anger to the exhaustion that comes from sleeplessness and sobbing. This loss and the renewed grief that you will feel is a long process, not one event.

Anything can trigger renewed grief because we are constantly reminded of our new world and the many ways we must adjust to living without our loved one. There is conflict in the midst of this change, and our body and mind react to this struggle.

A sudden, temporary upsurge of grief can happen for a number of reasons. Your reaction can come as a response to the anniversary of the death, a birthday, or another meaningful holiday. A favorite season that has special memories to either of you may bring back a wave of longing and grief.

Unexpected grief can be triggered because you reach an age that is associated with the death of your loved one. For example, when you celebrate your birthday but it means living more years than a sibling did, you may feel guilt along with renewed grief. An experience, such as a wedding or graduation, even if it comes decades after the loss, can trigger waves of grief response.

The loss of an invisible connection to a loved one may result in an upsurge of unresolved or new grief. The secondary loss of the pet of a deceased child, for example, may mean that the parents have lost a beloved animal as well as their most meaningful living reminder of what their child cared about. Understanding that each secondary loss requires its own time and response may help everyone to adjust their expectations and use more patience during these unexpected periods of grief. When we do not work through the additional losses that arise out of the primary death our grief may become prolonged.

Temporary Exaggerations of Grief . . .

Emerge during a meaningful life cycle, time, or stimulus:

- Anniversary (birthday, death, marriage)
- Holiday
- Season
- Ritual (wedding, birth, baptism)
- Coming-of-age marker (bar mitzvah, graduation)
- Reunion
- Memory-induced
- Music-elicited
- Sensory-induced (food, clothing, scents)

❧ ❥ ❧

Grieving Is Acknowledged through Rituals and in Keepsakes

It is a common fear of survivors that their loved one will be forgotten. That fear can result in prolonged grief and holding on to our loved one, or her story, because of the belief that everyone else has let go. The irrational fear is that if we loosen the grip on our grief, we will forget our loved one. A healthier response is to create rituals and ceremonies in which our loved one can be remembered and celebrated, and the reality of his death can be acknowledged.

Rituals provide us structure and language to deal with the enormous change in our lives. They underscore the finality and truth of death, helping us to begin the work of accepting the reality. Rituals set aside the time and context to express the feelings surrounding our loss, and they legitimize and confirm our relationship with the deceased, her importance in our life, and our place in her life. Rituals gather support for the survivors and identify them as people in transition.

Generations ago, family members shared the rituals of cleaning, dressing, and preparing the deceased for burial; designing and building a coffin; and digging the burial plot as ways to accept the reality of separation while continuing to care for their loved one. The ritual of a funeral service brings people together to celebrate the life and importance of the deceased; mourners say his name, remember shared life experiences, and put words to collective feelings. Sending a card to a survivor on the anniversary of their parent's death is a ritual that acknowledges the ongoing nature of grief, and it relieves the mourner of her fear that her loved one might be forgotten.

Year after year I go out into the ocean, where my mother's and father's ashes were spread, to reexamine my grief, to review their lives, and to spend time in silent gratitude. Any dedicated time or demonstration of the relationship is a mark of a ritual, and the provisions or tools used within rituals connect participants to the deceased.

A keepsake is a physical memento or an image that connects the mourner in a comforting way to the deceased. It can help the mourner accept the reality of the death while maintaining a meaningful bond, at the same time transitioning and reinvesting energy into a life without the loved one.

A linking object is any object that belonged to the deceased and has meaning to the mourner, such as an award, jewelry, a letter, or a toy. It can also be made of any word or phrase that describes the character or core traits of the deceased. You might create a collage of words such as *joy*, *gratitude*, and *generosity* that represent your loved one's legacy. These words can be repeated as a soothing mantra during times of stress or profound longing. A keepsake can also be a symbol or a message that represents your feelings or acts as a summary of the relationship. You might laminate a special note that your child left you before he died, carrying it with you in your wallet as a linking object. A linking object is any tangible property that has connection or meaning to the deceased's life or evokes her presence. It is not viewed as a substitute for the loved one, so if the object were lost, another of the same or different representation can be equally comforting. A linking object might be a small patch from his mother's sweater to remind a son of her warmth. A linking object, transitional object, or keepsake can be carried around for years to validate a person's inner experience that though his loved one is dead, they are still connected. Over time, linking objects may become less necessary or powerful as the mourner adjusts to life without the loved one.

There is no such thing as closure, but there is potential for healing. Grief is extremely personal, not a linear, step-by-step process. Grief is a long-term undertaking that can reappear at any time and ask to be reworked. The question we usually ask is *Will I ever get over it?*, and the answer is yes—and no. We can reach a time when remembering does not overwhelm us as it did in the beginning. We heal, but we remember, and living with the memory is part of the healing.

Thoughts of *What if?* are another way of circling around the reality of our loved one's death; we continue to consider what is lost and how our life is different. This is the acknowledgment and reaffirmation of so great a loss. We continue to grieve and acknowledge the many reasons for that grief. It is important to continue to acknowledge the difference your loved one's death makes in your life. Often when we let the feelings swell, verbalize them, and have them affirmed, we can then begin to step forward again.

Grief is a wound on every dimension of our being, and it needs attention in order to heal. The emotional, spiritual, and cognitive scar tissue is evidence of the change in our lives. To attend to our grief is to stay open and vulnerable to the feelings that arise, to express them in our authentic ways, and to respond to the feelings and needs as they resurface. The wounds of grief do heal. As we treat our grief in all dimensions, we heal and integrate, making the wound a part of the whole. That scar becomes woven into the body and becomes stronger than the original tissue. We can be scarred but healed—and stronger for it.

7

WE EACH GRIEVE IN UNIQUE WAYS

It was [his] life that was over, not mine. I had to remember that
recognizing the distinction was not disloyalty.

ELIZABETH BERG, *THE YEAR OF PLEASURES*

Each person experiences loss and expresses grief unlike anyone else. Each grief is like a snowflake. Though a person may have had several losses, each becomes a grief that is unlike any other. Factors such as a person's background, history with the dying person, culture, and experience as well as the mode of death and the meaning of the loss all define and may complicate grief. No two deaths can be compared.

Do not judge your feelings during your grief; do not judge the intensity, duration, or expression of your emotions. No one should assume anything about a person's relationship with the dying. Bereavement is the state of deprivation following the loss of someone or something that is significant; the relationship may be positive or negative, but grief is still experienced. Labels about the familial connection between two people do not accurately describe the meaning or the value of the relationship. In other words, one daughter may not feel the same intensity of grief as her sibling after the death of their mother because the history and attachment between the children and their dying mother is unique to each relationship. Each person has his own complex set of personality traits, history, values, and previous losses that affect how grief will be felt and understood. We must not impose our expectations for response, reactions, and expression toward the dying because we do not fully understand the bond between individuals.

Factors That Determine Each Person's Unique Grieving Process

- The coping strategies learned in life before the death
- The experiences she has had with prior deaths
- The quality and meaning of her relationship with the deceased
- The circumstances of the death:
  - Sudden and unexpected
  - Physical trauma
  - Length of time to adapt to the loss
- Religious beliefs and customs
- Personality traits and attitudes
- The emotional support from family and friends
- The meaning attributed to the death

Grief Is Normal

Grief is not a disease. Grief is not pathology. Grief is not an illness to be cured. Grief is different than depression. When we are grieving, it is common to feel dejected, to lose interest in the outside world, and to pull inward, but we can still respond to social outreach and compassion. Grief symptoms usually soften within a year as survivors learn to adjust to and find meaning in a world without their loved one.

The symptoms of depression may worsen over time without intervention. Depression leads us to say, "I am worthless" and "I am a bad person for feeling sad." Those who are depressed may feel dejected and rejected but blame themselves. They carry anger toward themselves and often unresolved anger toward the deceased, whether they are conscious of it or not. They often reject social contact and support. Their activity in the outside world is more likely paralyzed than inhibited. Grief needs validation; depression warrants psychotherapy or medication or both.

Grief Is Universal

All living things with a brain stem experience grief. Grief is a common, collective experience shared by all humans and animals. Grief is experienced whether one is intelligent or developmentally delayed, an infant or an elder. A six-year-old with Down syndrome grieves the death of her sister; an eighty-year-old with Alzheimer's grieves the death of his dog; a young mother grieves the loss of her three-month-old fetus; and a young teenage boy grieves the death of his team coach. Grief is about the attachment to someone or something of value.

Grief Is a Yearning

We grieve when we lose an attachment. Our psyche protests the loss of the connection we once had, the loss of the loved one who is gone. If we are to resume healthy lives and healthy relationships, we cannot deny the reality or the pain of our loss. We must come to understand what the loss of this person and the relationship means to our life. We must learn to build a new world without this person or the structure of this relationship. It takes time to adjust and a period of confusion before we learn how to live in a world without our loved one. We wrestle with new questions such as *Who am I now?* as we learn to live without the relationship the loved one provided.

Grief Is Work

Grief is active. No one can do your grief work for you. Healthy grief work is repeated until one finds resolution. No roadmap will preclude the repetitive struggles and requirements of grief. Thoughts of the deceased person preoccupy us. We must revisit the loss over and over in our mind and feel the pain. We must struggle to explain the loss, make sense of events, and find meaning in our loved one's death. All of this takes time, effort, energy, and repetition.

Grief work is repetitious and dynamic. It changes throughout our lifetime, revealing itself in unexpected surges of emotion. Grief can be like a jack-in-the-box—we never know when it will raise its shocking or scary head again. A meaningful song can trigger grief; a special season of the year, a birthday or anniversary, the scent of a special perfume, or the bite of a favorite cookie may all bring back a great wave of grief. It can feel overwhelming and unmanageable for its unpredictability. But the sudden surges of grief are temporary and normal, all part of the healthy coping process of grief.

Grief Work Is the Process of Adjusting and Adapting

Grief work takes time. Death, loss, and grief are not one-dimensional or linear. When we suffer loss, we do not go through the grief work just once, in a straight line. Grief comes in waves and surges, repeatedly, and with different intensities through a lifetime. It does not end, but it can soften. Grief becomes unhealthy only when a person becomes stuck in it and cannot adjust to the reality of the death. Ongoing, unresolved grief leads to a diminished life.

It is helpful to recognize grief by its different domains so we can identify the ways that grief is working its way through us. Grief is experienced and expressed in the physical, cognitive, emotional, spiritual, and relationship domains. After a loss, one can expect to have difficulty coping with a variety of practical, social, economic, and spiritual matters that might affect their functioning in the world. When we go through the long trek of grief, we can feel exhausted in every area of our life.

Grief Is Experienced in the Body

Our heart aches. Our stomach hurts. Our throat closes up. Our joints ache. This is normal grief, rather than illness, experienced anytime after a loss. This may be the first or primary way that a young person is able to tell an adult about his feelings of grief. We can help him make sense of his feelings when we translate his physical sensations into words that explain his sensations surrounding his grief.

Your grief witnesses a ruptured life, and your body expresses what it perceives. Grief feels disinterested in life, numb in the body; grief is exhausting, disturbing, confusing; grief is up and down, disorienting.

Your whole life may feel stuck, and your body may feel blocked. The blocked state that you are experiencing may be your body's way of gently managing a torrent of changes that would otherwise be too sudden and too overwhelming, and would make you too vulnerable. This blocked state may be modulating the intensity of emotion and degree of shock so that you can cope. I believe there is a deep and sacred wisdom of the body that is often more skilled and adaptive than the prescriptions of our mind, which are influenced by social norms and expectations, not always in our best interest.

Physical Responses to Grief

Tightness in chest or throat   Muscle weakness
Oversensitivity to noise   Dry mouth

Shortness of breath	Hollowness in stomach
Lack of energy	Sense of depersonalization

Grief Affects Our Behavior

Our bodies respond to the pain of separation from a loved one and express it through chemical and physiological changes and adjustment. Grief is biological and is demonstrated through the different ways of protesting, seeking, and detaching. When we are stressed or suffering from emotional pain, we operate from the more instinctive, mammalian middle brain. The executive functioning part of the brain that is responsible for analysis, adaptation, empathy, and future planning shuts down. Our brains and bodies adjust to a survival mode as we try to regain control. This is why you may notice that it is difficult to focus and concentrate, read a book for more than a few pages, or recall what was just said to you. Give yourself permission to take time. Acknowledge that it may take many months before you are physically and cognitively able to return to your previous level of activity or involvement at work, or with others.

Behavioral Responses to Grief

- Sleep disturbance, including too much or too little
- Appetite disturbance resulting in over- or undereating
- Avoiding reminders of the deceased
- Searching and calling out
- Visiting places as reminders of the deceased

- Restless overactivity
- Saving objects of the deceased
- Crying
- Sighing

Grief Is Processed Cognitively

As mourners, we acknowledge a death only after understanding the reality of the death through facts and circumstances. This process takes time. We recognize grief in the ways that it shows itself as confusion, disorientation, lack of focus, and the inability to read or remember. During grief, the left hemisphere of the brain where language is formed lies dormant and still. We find we have a difficult time verbally expressing our pain: "I just can't talk about it."

Our right brain is the grieving brain, and it holds the images of the death that we see over and over again as we work through our grief. It is helpful to connect both hemispheres of the brain through activities such as art therapy, dance therapy, and/or music therapy to express the pain in nonverbal ways. Asking a sixteen-year-old guitar player whose mother died, "How does your pain sound?" might help him give form to his feelings and help him to later verbalize his grief. Providing crayons and paper to a six-year-old would help her illustrate her feelings and thoughts that she does not yet have language for.

Thoughts of Grief

Disbelief	Confusion
Pessimism	Poor comprehension

Aimlessness
Distraction
Obsession
Poor decision making
Disorganization

Denial
Bewilderment
Impaired concentration
Rumination

Grief Is Emotional

We rant, rave, and fight against loss. Emotionally we may feel insecure, overwhelmed, and angry. Grief feels like a loss of security, and when we lose the person who helped us know our best self, we may forget temporarily who we are in the world. We lose our confidence and are unsure about what we can count on in a world that is always changing and full of loss.

Emotions of Grief

Sadness	Anger	Intolerance
Anguish	Impatience	Guilt
Anxiety	Regret	Hopelessness
Panic	Frustration	Loneliness
Fear	Abandonment	Ambivalence
Insecurity	Relief	Overwhelm
Yearning	Helplessness	Powerlessness
Craziness	Apathy	Hypersensitivity

Grief Is Spiritual

The spiritual aspects of dying and grieving relate to the way we seek and express meaning during dying, death, and grieving. We must attend to the spiritual need of experiencing connectedness to ourselves, to others, to the dying, and to the sacred. We must find meaning in whatever we experience through the death and in our grief. If you or another mourner is struggling to reorganize your world after a loss, find a metaphor and a way of understanding death that helps you reconcile the enormous change in your life. Thoughts such as *I feel useless, My life is meaningless, God has abandoned me,* and *My loved one should not have suffered* are all existential statements concerned with finding meaning.

As caregivers to the bereaved, we must attend to spiritual distress in the same way as other medical challenges. We must intervene with compassionate presence, skillful listening, and meaning-oriented strategies to address spiritual values, beliefs, and practices. Interventions such as massage, visualization, mindfulness meditation, life review, religious contemplation, and referral for spiritual care all have a place before, during, and after death. When individuals practice these relaxation and centering techniques, they are more able to connect with others, achieve calm and peaceful attention, develop a heightened intuition, and renew and balance their whole being.

Spiritual Reactions to Grief

- Anger
- Spiritual confusion
- Alienation from God
- Increased spirituality

- Paranormal experiences pertaining to the deceased (such as a sense of the deceased's presence or after-death communication)
- Loss of order
- Loss of meaning
- Hopelessness
- Loss of faith

Grief Is Not a Reflection of How Well We Loved

Grief is a love story, and as such it is unique and personal, often internal and private. Love and grief take many forms and are expressed in many ways. None of these outward signs of mourning are the same as the inner experience. Likewise, outward demonstrations of grief are not an indication of the intensity of the loss, nor is the expression of our grief an accurate reflection of the value of the person who is dying.

We must be sensitive to differing personal styles and expressions of grief, careful not to judge or compare one person's grief expression to another's. Any two individuals grieving the loss of the same person may have difficulty accepting and reconciling their differences in grief expression. For example, couples often have difficulty accepting and reconciling these differences; a daughter may be more verbal and vocal than a brother after the death of a parent while both share intense sadness and a similar understanding of what it means to be in a world without their mentor and spiritual anchor. If a father contains his grief more stoically and silently than the mother of a deceased child, it must not be interpreted to mean that he feels less toward his child. We must honor all grief, visible or invisible, vocal or silent. The expressions of grief and the ways that grief is experienced are affected by several factors.

Grief Depends on the Circumstances of the Loss

A traumatic death is sudden, unanticipated, random, and sometimes violent. Sudden or traumatic death may be the most difficult loss to adjust to; it does not make sense, and it happens without the opportunity to prepare, say good-bye, finish business, or adjust to the change in our lives. Homicide, suicide, car accidents, strokes, heart attacks, and anaphylactic reactions may intensify survivors' reactions of anxiety or guilt. Traumatic losses may cause an existential crisis as survivors struggle to find meaning and reevaluate their belief systems and values. What might be considered a timely or more age-expected death of an elderly loved one fits into our cultural understanding of the life cycle, and it may be easier to understand and reconcile.

The nature, or perceived value, of the attachment to the person makes a difference to the intensity of our experience. The meaning of the relationship affects our grief. The perceived need of the deceased to the survivor impacts and influences the grief outcome. For example, the death of a caregiver, whether a parent or another trusted adult, to a child screams of the loss of security, safety, and a place in the world. "Who will take care of me?" and "Will I be okay?" are typical reactions when a child receives news that a parent has died. A child's dependence on adults for survival makes the surviving parent's ability to cope with his own grief as well as his ability to provide the emotional, psychological, and physical continuity of care of paramount importance. With the healthy, consistent attention from one responsible adult, most children adjust to death and become resilient. In addition, children's grief support groups are shown to have the best therapeutic outcomes for grieving children, especially when combined with individual counseling and art therapies for expression.

The loss of a child in Western society is much more rare today than it was fifty years ago, and the anomaly adds to the overwhelming reaction people often experience. The death of a child disrupts powerful biological, psychological, and social needs for survival, kinship, and caregiving. A child's death may mean the end of future dreams and a legacy for parents; metaphorically, it may feel like an amputation. The death of a child brings chaos to the natural expectation that the elderly will decline before young people do, and this can change the way parents identify themselves and their place in the world.

"I didn't do my job," "I'm a failure," and "I didn't protect my child" are common responses after the death of a child, no matter what age. Parents' inner experience may be guilt, shame, helplessness, and frustration; as they repeatedly try to make sense of the death, they may take on the responsibility as a way of bringing a false sense of order into what feels like a chaotic world. As their world changes, parents must modify and reorganize their worldview to successfully answer their questions about their place and power in their world. The death of a child results in a complex and multifaceted grief. The place that the child held in life is often replaced by a preoccupation with the child, the death event, and feelings of guilt and sadness that may ebb and flow through the years. Some couples' relationships break down under the lengthy stress of mourning a child, while others are strengthened and solidified.

The history of the relationship also affects the experience and the expression of grief. The history of the attachment may have been long, loving, and supportive. When a spouse has lost such a relationship, her response might be "I do not know how to live without my husband," while another bereaved wife might react with "He filled my life, and I don't need another relationship." The circumstances, history, and meaning of the relationship to the surviving loved one guide our grief work. We cannot presume to know how people will interpret loss and how they will adjust to their future without their loved one.

Each person approaches grief with his or her own set of strengths and challenges. We should all be encouraged to be authentic and to remain in character through grief. Each of us comes with a history and a way of seeing the world that sets him or her apart from anyone else coping with the same loss. We must not set standards for the pace of grief or for its intensity, demonstration, or verbalization.

We learn coping strategies through previous losses, such as the physical death of a person or the symbolic loss of a life dream. Previous losses help develop skills and competencies, attitudes and confidence, but they cannot delay or diminish the work of each subsequent loss. However, death competencies and the confidence to be around death diminish fear, anxiety, and regret, thus significantly reducing complicated and unresolved grief.

Grief Is Shaped by Our Culture and Levels of Social Support

Our culture teaches us how to grieve, and it gives us both subtle and direct messages about death and grief. Cultures are death accepting, death denying, or death defying. Whether we accept or deny the process of dying, the lengthy work of grief and our changed world as a survivor is related to where and with whom we were raised.

We view and respond to death as sacred or profane; our language, customs, and attitudes reflect our cultural education. If we receive subtle or indirect messages that our grief is not okay, we are more likely to grieve in silence, isolated from others who could support us. Grief may not be sanctioned, recognized, or encouraged in cases of suicide or in which a perceived blame is placed upon the deceased. Religious or political views also create barriers to grief, as in the case of abortion or illnesses like AIDS.

When there is something dishonorable or unusual about the relationship with the dying person, or the nature of the death, mourners are often left unattended, stigmatized, or dismissed. An unacknowledged or disenfranchised death such as miscarriage or suicide may receive little or no social support, ritual, or honor, making it one of the more difficult losses to come to terms with. Similarly, when someone loses a former spouse, a stillborn fetus, or a demented parent, the unwillingness to acknowledge and offer social support may intensify feelings of abandonment, guilt, shame, and alienation.

Problematic Social Responses to Grief

- New difficulties in interpersonal relationships
- Problems functioning in a group
- No longer belonging to or identifying with a past support system
- Perceiving self as a third wheel, a burden
- Jealous feelings toward other couples or families

Expressions of grief are not random; they develop out of societal and cultural ways of understanding the world. Loss has different meanings from culture to culture. Indigenous people in different corners of the world have long-standing rituals and customs to help them understand and find meaning in death. Grief is accepted and woven into daily life in such a way that it serves as a teacher. For example, one Native American practice during grief is to cut a mourner's long braid as a sign that a part of her is missing. It is also a reminder to her, as her hair grows back, that life continues and healing is a part of life.

People respond to loss and cope with grief in ways that protect themselves, family, and society. For example, Anglican cultures tend to experience and speak of grief in psychological terms, whereas other cultures tend to experience and speak of their grief in physical terms. Some cultures sanction wailing and demonstrative outpouring of grief, while others feel strongly that it is unseemly to expose such intense emotions.

Grief is often misunderstood, especially between cultures. People of one group may believe that a mourner should have moved on within three months after a loved one's death. If the bereaved receive that message or are working under the same misguided framework, the work of grief is complicated by disapproval. *I'm crazy* or *I'm depressed* are burdensome labels that impede healthy mourning.

Our families make it easier to grieve when we are taught language and methods for expressing our grief within the setting that supports us. Families that make it a practice to discuss the subject of illness, death, and dying as part of normal life help family members prepare and normalize what will be part of their future. When parents talk with their children about death and dying, they can normalize dying and relieve suffering. Families can acknowledge the pain of loss, but as they offer support and validation, they also transform the experience from suffering to a major milestone of life.

Grief Has Masculine and Feminine Expressions

Although grief can be masculine or feminine, this does not mean that males always grieve differently than females. Rather, there are different styles of expressing or demonstrating grief that take on characteristics that can be viewed as masculine or feminine. There are masculine and feminine strategies for coping, and these are differences rather than deficiencies.

It is important to acknowledge, encourage, and support whatever style of grief and strategy for coping a person is able to work with. Women may have a masculine grief style, keeping their emotions to themselves, while men may be more comfortable with the verbally expressive and open, feminine style of grieving. While most people are more adept or comfortable with one style of expression over another, a person's grief style may change or include both masculine and feminine aspects. The path toward either style of grief is determined by our socialization, maturity and age, culture, and previous experiences.

Jacqueline Kennedy demonstrated a more masculine style of grief that was private, quiet, and externalized by building memorials and programs to remember her husband. C. S. Lewis had a more feminine coping strategy by externalizing his grief and sharing it with others; he was a gifted writer who worked through and expressed his grief in his writing and speaking. Both styles are healthy when they help the mourner move through the tasks and processes of grief work. However, either strategy may complicate grief work if it is used to avoid the reality or feelings of the loss.

This is an important validation for masculine mourners because our Western culture tends to endorse and support feminine styles of grief. More research has been reported on widows and mothers, and most therapies are designed for women who tend to verbalize their feelings. Consequently, I often counsel couples who have differing styles and expressions of their grief. They are suspicious and judgmental about each other's experience of grief at a time when they most need to support each other. The husband most often reports feeling criticized because he does not talk about his feelings and does not cry as openly as his wife. His wife interprets this to mean that he did not love their deceased child as she believed, and she begins to question his character and value as a man. Meanwhile, the husband may feel that his wife is too dramatic with her grief. Therapists, too, may experience that the partner who displays a masculine style of grief is difficult to work with, the partner encouraging only the verbal expression of grief.

As caregivers to the bereaved, rather than comparing or judging his grief style and coping strategies, it is helpful to understand his orientation toward masculine or feminine grieving processes so we can support his grief work. To assess whether a mourner has a masculine grief orientation, we should look at his level of movement and activity. Masculine-style grief is action-oriented and problem-focused versus emotion-focused and person-centered. The masculine mourner engages in activities to restore life to balance and order; this mourner attends to new tasks, distracts himself from his grief through actively engaging in projects or movement, and works at developing a new role and new relationships. Masculine grieving is facilitated when he is given a map of sorts, with resources about what to do, how to do it, and when it will end. If the masculine mourner is encouraged to be in touch with his body and essentially sweat his tears, he will find himself successfully working through the tasks of grief.

A masculine griever talks about his loss in relation to his body; "My stomach hurts" or "I have a heaviness in my chest" describes his grief accurately. Masculine grief work might involve designing and building a new fence after his daughter's fatal car accident, where she was crushed against an old fence. Masculine grief often builds and maintains memorials.

Our Western culture expects and supports the feminine grief style and coping strategies. The feminine style of grief is outwardly expressive. We know a feminine mourner's grief through her words and tears. She shares readily and already has support systems in place because she is accustomed to sharing. Her descriptions of her grief are in terms of her feelings; "I feel overwhelmed" or "I feel guilty" helps explain her grief. The outward sharing also helps to maintain her connection to others and her need for intimacy. Her participation does not have the same end place that masculine grievers require; however, because of this, talking about her grief may keep a person stuck in the task of feeling the emotions instead of moving toward finding meaning in the loss. The key to supporting either style of grief expression is to honor and acknowledge different paths of healing.

Characteristics of Masculine Grief Orientation

Autonomous	Action-oriented
Independent	Outcome-oriented

Private   Focused on an end in sight
Orderly   Geared toward creating a product
Quiet

Interventions to Masculine Grief

- Humor
- Reading a book for information
- Cognitive organization; understanding
- Looking at a picture album
- Creating a product: building a bench, organizing a race, making a video, raising money for a scholarship fund
- Rituals to maintain solitude

Characteristics of Feminine Grief Orientation

Relational   Verbal
Open   Feeling-oriented
Intimate   Ongoing, repetitive

Interventions to Feminine Grief

- Support groups
- Storytelling
- Crying
- Retelling, "Every death deserves a hundred tellings"[1]

- Grief counseling
- Writing, singing, emailing
- Public rituals

Grief Work Is Recognized in Different Ways

There are different ways of knowing grief. It is helpful to understand these methods and recognize that you are accomplishing the necessary work after the loss of a loved one. You can conceptualize grief work in phases, tasks, and processes. You may recognize yourself, or someone you are accompanying through grief, in one or several of the following descriptions. It is reassuring to put words to what is being experienced.

We can recognize grief reactions as phases that we work through. Even if we have anticipated death because we have been preparing through an extended illness, the loss of a loved one leaves us shocked. Our world feels out of balance without our loved one. The numbing effect is our body's way of helping us cope. We may find ourselves sure that we recognize our deceased loved one as we scan the shopping mall and see someone walking with exactly the same posture. We search; we yearn to see our loved one again. The world feels upside down, and nothing makes sense. We feel lost and without hope for a long time, until gradually, we find that we begin to make sense of ourselves in a new world. We find we are sleeping more, focusing longer, and staying on task. We accept that our loved one is not in our world, and we cope, day by day.

Phases of Grief

1. Shock and numbness

2. Yearning and searching for the loved one

3. Disorganization and despair

4. Reorganization

To recognize our grief work through tasks and processes is to understand grief in active verbs. This is work, and the work is repetitive. Repetitive thoughts, feelings, and actions are normal. They are our coping rhythms as we adjust to living in the world without our loved one. Repetitive reminiscences of the deceased are necessary in order to make sense and to create a new place for ourselves in the world. This is healthy grief.

When others are mourning, you can help by listening to the same story as many times as the mourner needs to tell it. She is trying to accept, adjust, and make sense of the sequence of events leading up to her loved one's death. She needs to revisit the story as though she is viewing a movie many times to be certain that the conclusion is the same.

We revisit each task or process over and over until we master the challenge. It may take a lifetime.

Tasks and Processes of Grief

Tasks and activities of grief can be sequential, overlapping,
and revisited repeatedly over a lifetime.

1. Accept the reality that your loved one is dead. Acknowledge the death and understand the facts.

2. Work through and feel the pain of grief. Give some form of expression to your reactions to the loss.

- Recollect and reexperience the deceased and the life you shared with him.
- React to separation from the loved one. Experience and feel the pain; give some form of expression to all the reactions to the loss (sing, write, cry, sweat, build, talk).

3. Adjust to the environment in which your loved one is not present. Move into a new world without forgetting the old.
   - Readjust to a new world while keeping a place within yourself for the deceased. Develop a new relationship with the deceased. Create new ways of being in the world, and develop a new identity without the deceased.
   - Reinvest energy in yourself, your new life, and your future.

4. Create an appropriate place for the deceased in their emotional and spiritual life; develop a different form of relationship with him that enables one to go on living satisfactorily in the world of the living.[2]

The resolution and acceptance of one's grief is always multifaceted and time-consuming. Grief work is active, and requires us to invest our energy and work through tasks. The bereaved must make sense of a new world without their loved one as they live through different developmental phases and life challenges, with different levels of support and resources.

NOTES

1. Hospice of the Monterey Peninsula, "Good Grief," Griefbusters program (Monterey, CA: Community Hospital of the Monterey Peninsula, 1985).

2. J. William Worden, *Grief Counseling and Grief Therapy: A Handbook for the Mental Health Practitioner, 4th ed.* (New York: Springer, 2008), 39–52.

8

CHILDREN GRIEVE DIFFERENTLY THAN ADULTS

Your children get only one childhood.

REGINA BRETT, *THE PLAIN DEALER*

Through our mother's illness and death, my brothers and I needed information, emotional support, and guidance. We were crippled without answers to questions we were afraid to ask, without the foundation of facts, and without time to prepare for such a void in our future. Without the gift of preparation, my mother's death felt random and capricious. Our sense of safety and control was shattered, and a sense of guilt replaced the carefree opportunities of childhood. My mother's death was acknowledged when it happened, but as a family we sidestepped talking about the reality and what it meant to us, avoiding any mention of her or our feelings after her absence.

The experience of my brothers and me is repeated all over the world, every day, when families do not know what to say to grieving children or how to respond to their needs. While conscientiously trying to manage their own grief, adults often underestimate the intensity and duration of children's grief. Thoughts and comments such as "She's only three years old; she'll forget these feelings," or "He's a tough little guy; he's resilient," do not address the fact that grief is about *feeling* deprived of someone or something of value. When the person to whom they were attached is removed through death, children feel the separation and deprivation. Children grieve whether or not they understand the details or concepts of death.

When we help children cope and learn from their grief, we help them mature into contributing members of a community that cares for others. As we help them understand the concepts of death, developing a realistic acceptance rather than a magical thinking about death, we accelerate resolution and healing. When we help develop children's emotional capacity for coping, they—as well as their family and community—benefit from the compassion and competency that they learn. When we assist children with their grief, we help them develop values. When we explain what matters, we teach our values, which in turn guides children to principles in action. We provide the next generation with a road map and the tools with which to navigate the challenges inherent in living. This infrastructure provides resources that build confidence and competency, and dispels unnecessary fears about the inevitable losses in life. Together, we build a future network of resources with which to cope and move toward a future, rather than a barricade that directs us toward fear of inevitable losses in life.

Children Need Help Understanding Death and Dying

Forty percent of all children will experience at least one traumatic event before they become adults.[1] It is estimated that 26 percent of children in the United States will witness or experience a traumatic event before the age of four.[2] A sense of trauma can come from the loss of anything that is significant to them, such as a friendship, a sense of safety, a pet, or a home, but grief is usually associated with the death of a loved one.[3]

Death, loss, and trauma are common experiences for children, but the challenge is usually not addressed until after the crisis has occurred. The opportunities for growth embedded within the crisis are too important to leave as afterthoughts. When we do not prepare our children with the skills or support to deal with personal change of this magnitude, the ramifications are dangerous. Adjustment disorders, behavioral problems, psychological distress, and psychosomatic illness can be the outcome of the lack of support, information, and modeling. As adults and caregivers, we need to discuss the inevitability of loss with children and teach them coping skills before they are needed, during a time that is not so emotionally volatile. When children are not taught life skills to manage and make sense of their emotions, dysfunctional responses such as suicide, addiction, and arrested development may be their response. Children need help if they are to navigate and successfully adjust to circumstances they do not understand and for which they have not developed skills.

Children Need Significant Support as They Deal with Loss

Without consistent assistance, children may carry scars of grief that impact their physical, emotional, and spiritual health as well as their relationships with others. They may not receive the emotional support or skills from primary adults if those adults are preoccupied with their own grief. In those circumstances, adults and caregivers other than parents can advance to the primary role. These people may include a pastor, a favorite teacher, a counselor, a neighbor, or a relative. All interventions and supportive activities help a child move toward the tasks of accepting the death. The goal is to help them learn to live in a world without the loved one and to become resilient.

Children's Reactions to Loss Are Always Changing

Child development is influenced by children's life experience, their exposure to events and people, their personality, and their culture. It is important as adult role models that we continue to check children's changing understanding of the different concepts of grief. Children's natural egocentricity leads to skewed and potentially damaging perspectives about dying and death. For example, a child may take on the responsibility for a parent's death, believing they have magical powers. Or a child who was jealous of his deceased sibling may exaggerate his personal power, believing he could have stopped a terminal illness. Without facts and context, children fill the voids of information with misunderstanding.

Developmental concepts of death are learned over time. Although there is disagreement among researchers, the general consensus at present is that most children develop the capacity to grieve between three and four years of age and continue as maturation occurs.

In order to fully understand the concept of death, a child must grasp five key subconcepts.

Five Subconcepts of Death

Universality

- All things die.
- No living thing can avoid death.
- Death is unpredictable.

Irreversibility

- Death is permanent.

Nonfunctionality

- Externally, actions like breathing, eating, walking, and playing stop.
- Internally, thinking, feeling, and dreaming cease.

Causality

- Certain external events lead to death.
- Specific internal events can cause death.

Continued Life Form

- We have some kind of internal representation of the person.
- We have some idea where they are.
- We have a level of continued relationship with the deceased.

Children Grieve in Ways That are Both Different from and Similar to Adults

Both children and adults must accept the reality of their loved one's death, work through their feelings, and come to a personal understanding about the meaning of the loss. But children have a range of understandings about the specific concepts of death that differs from that of the mature adult with life experience.

The age and life experience of children directly affect their grief reactions and responses. Children work through different developmental phases of understanding, insight, and adjustment to the concepts of death. A young child has not yet developed the ability to understand that death is irreversible and final. A child who is four or five years of age may still believe that he has the power to cause death to happen, and he will have to work through the guilt associated with that magical thinking. Children commonly perceive events around them as under their control and, thus, a natural death as their fault. Rationalizations include *Mommy went away and died because I did not pick up my toys; if I had picked up my toys, I could have stopped her death.* Older children with experience of adjusting to a pet's death, a school transfer, or the loss of a best friend are more able to cope when their loved one dies. As a child works through the tasks and understanding of his grief, he is developing cognitively, emotionally, psychologically, and behaviorally. A child can benefit from different kinds of support, such as less verbally challenging activities of art, play, music, drama, and dance.

Children's experience with illness and their exposure to someone in the dying process are usually limited in our culture. We are more likely to handle dying needs in a hospital than within our home as past generations did. Children do not see or understand the progression of an illness and therefore are not able to adjust to loss gradually.

Without an understanding of the progression and reality of a terminal illness, children are deprived of the opportunity to prepare for the death, adjust to a different future, or say good-bye in a personally meaningful way. Instead, children will react to what they perceive as a secretive death as they would to a sudden, unexpected loss. The normal reactions of shock and disbelief are exaggerated and include feelings of guilt, regret, helplessness, anger, and hopelessness. To mitigate these reactions, a significant adult needs to provide emotional support, nurturance, and consistency.

Children do not have the vocabulary or expressive ability to share their thoughts and feelings about their grief. They may be experiencing confusion related to the loss of a parent, but they do not have the language, skills, experience, or confidence to share their grief with others. This leaves them vulnerable to misunderstanding, judgment, and isolation. After my mother's death, alone with my thoughts and fantasies, I pieced together a story to explain to myself what had happened and why. I did not know how to check my understanding against solid information that an adult held. Lost in my confusion and in the struggle to understand, I created more pain for myself.

With limited skills and experience with which to ask for help, children often do not know that support systems and designated community resources exist, nor do they know how to seek them out. A child in need does not have the connections to others who have skillfully navigated through a similar upheaval. When children are afraid or their sense of security is threatened, they tend to isolate and withdraw, or they may lash out and then regress.

Children are rarely encouraged to participate in the care of a dying loved one. It is more common to seclude the dying family member and refrain from incorporating the child into the process. When children are not included or offered understanding, the death is a mystery; it becomes a death without any physical evidence, as in a plane crash, and children are left with lingering hope and expectation that there has been a mistake. Even at thirteen years old, because I did not see my mother or her body after she left for the hospital, I made up stories that she had just gone away and would return one day.

However, if children are included in the opportunities to care for the dying person, are taught how to participate, and are supported as they interact, there are opportunities for growth and healing for everyone. Children can be included first through appropriate, age-based information about the illness and prognosis; information alleviates, rather than accentuates, fear and anxiety in children. Simple physical chores such as applying body lotion, swabbing chapped lips, refreshing water bottles, and physically companioning their loved one are activities that are appropriate and empowering. As I worked through my feelings of grief, remembering that I had helped my mother by preparing a simple meal the last time I saw her softened my feelings of regret and guilt.

The youngest members of the family are often discouraged from participating in planning or attending rituals surrounding death. Many families do not know when or how to include a child in one of life's most natural and normal milestones. Children should be given a choice to attend the ritual, and provisions should be made according to the child's age and attention span. Arrange for a close friend to take children home if a ceremony taxes the children in any way. Children need to be prepared for what they will see, hear, and experience. Explain what will be done with the body when it no longer works; describe where the body or ashes will be stored, and be sure to tell the child if the casket will be open. Children should be given information about where the burial site is so they can visit if they want to. This also serves to help them understand that their loved one no longer has a viable body. Tell them what will happen in the funeral home and at the cemetery or site where the ashes are stored or released. Rehearse with children and take them to the site of the funeral ritual beforehand if possible. Help them participate in the funeral ritual at the level that they are able and willing to play a part; participation builds support and understanding while lessening fear and anxiety. Funeral planning and participation help children feel important and useful at a time when they would otherwise feel overwhelmed and helpless.

When one of my patients passed on, I asked his six-year-old son, Tyler, how he would like to say good-bye to his father at the funeral. His mother was surprised, but relieved, to hear Tyler say that he wanted to draw a picture and tie it to a helium balloon to be released into the air outside the church. In another experience, nine-year-old Tammy felt she was able to comfort her older brother who had died because she was asked how she wanted to be involved; she decided to give her favorite stuffed animal as a gift to be included in her brother's coffin.

Children and adults share common needs, experiences, and responses to death. All people in grief need safety in order to gather the demanding energy required to accept, understand, and integrate their loss. Both children and adults need the physical and emotional safety of time, space, and respect to move through the work of grief. Children's grief can be supported when we set aside a special place, what I like to call a grieving fort, where they can feel contained and emotionally safe. Encouraging a child to set aside time each day or week to draw a picture of their feelings shows respect and acknowledgment for the way they choose to express their grief.

Children, as well as adults, have a wide range of ways that they express their grief. All expressions are ways of externalizing one's emotions and moving them out of the body to reduce stress. Children, like adults, have differing ways of knowing themselves and expressing their understanding of what has happened. All forms of expressing grief—whether they are verbal or physical and manifested through something like singing or art—need to be encouraged and honored.

Both children and adults feel grief before, during, and after the death of a loved one. Even when accurate information is withheld, children and adults usually have an intuitive level of awareness about their loved one or what is happening, but they may not be able to express it directly. The intuitive grief about an undisclosed illness or death may be expressed as confusion, anger, resentment, and withdrawal. Being aware of reactions and appropriately responding throughout the course of loss will bring opportunities for children to develop coping skills and garner the support needed.

Both children and adults reexperience and revisit their grief throughout their lifetime. Their understanding about the loss, their process to create meaning, and their ability to cope with the reality change as they mature. Both children and adults work through the layers of loss across their lifetime, depending on their available resources as well as their skills, abilities, and support systems. Grief reemerges throughout a lifetime; it is never closed but integrated into life. Sudden temporary upsurges of grief are a normal part of the healing process, and children should be taught this.

Children, like adults, grieve physically, emotionally, cognitively, and spiritually. We must not assume that children do not experience grief on each level merely because they lack the expressive ability to let us know. A child's needs on every level must be attended to and supported.

How to Help a Child Understand Death

- Listen actively to learn what the child does and does not understand about death. Listen for the vocabulary and concepts she is able to use in questions or descriptions of the events.
- Ask the child direct, simple questions that focus on the five subconcepts needed for full understanding.
- Respond to what he does and does not understand.
- Use everyday living experiences and teaching moments to discuss the reality that has happened.
- Answer questions when the child asks. Answer simply and honestly rather than evading the truth in an effort to protect her from a harsh reality.
- Temper your responses to reflect the child's capacity for emotion and facts.
- Answer the question that is asked; do not overwhelm the child with detail, but ask him to paraphrase what you explained to see if he now understands.
- Give the child time alone to reflect.
- Provide opportunities and experiences for the child to show you what she understands or is confused about regarding illness, death, and dying.

Examples of How a Child Can Help

- An elementary-school-aged child can provide companionship by doing homework alongside the dying person and, when appropriate, including his loved one in the homework tasks.

- An eight- to twelve-year-old child can be responsible for supplying fresh water, arranging flowers for the room, or changing the pillowcase daily.
- A ten-year-old child can be a correspondent, writing letters dictated by the dying.
- A child old enough to read can be responsible for reading prescreened cards and letters that arrive.
- A child can apply hand lotion and massage dry skin on hands or feet.
- A child might be appointed to share a joke or to read a story each day.
- A child can inquire about and listen to a dying loved one's life stories.
- A child can play cards or watch television with her dying relative.

Children Need Constant Help Feeling and Expressing Their Emotions

Grieving children need guidance in order to find meaning in the loss. Activities provide a child with a person, place, and means of giving expression to their fears, needs, and feelings. Teaching moments allow a child to ask for and receive answers to their questions and concerns. Activities centered on the real issues of living and dying, and on our values and beliefs about life events, help to normalize loss, dying, and death as inevitable, universal, and normal parts of life.

Grieving children need to have their needs and questions responded to, at their level of understanding, as they arise. Helpful caregivers assess children's needs and questions while also recognizing what is not being asked or is not understood. Constant, consistent availability for grieving children means that they will be able to circle around to seek further support as new or higher-level needs and questions emerge. Constancy and consistency allow children to set the pace for healing so they are not overwhelmed with information or expectations, nor are their abilities to cope underestimated. Routines provide a sense of normalcy and give children an environment that can resemble what was healthy and safe before the loss.

We cannot leave grieving children alone with their grief or leave their work of grief to chance. Children need safety to explore and express their feelings. They need constant reassurance that any and all of their feelings are acceptable. Children need guidance to be able to choose healthy ways to express their feelings.

Children's Questions about the Subconcepts of Death

- Universality: Does everyone die? Do children die too? Can someone with superpowers get away from death?
- Irreversibility: How long do you stay dead after you die? Can Daddy come back?
- Nonfunctionality: What do you do when you're dead? How do dead people go to the bathroom? Do dead people get sad?
- Causality: Why do people die? Do people die because I wished it?
- Continued life form: Where do my thoughts go when I die? Is there a heaven?

Children Need Language to Express Grief

Children need words and images to accurately understand the concept of death and the event. Expressions such as *passed away, passed on,* or that someone *left us,* was *taken by God,* or has *gone to sleep* confuse children and create unnecessary anxiety. Indirect language that soft-peddles the finality and causality of death does not help grieving children understand or learn how to cope with the reality. When we explain to a child that someone died and then ask him what he understands that to mean, we give ourselves the opportunity to explain and expand based on their level of understanding.

When we must report to a four-year-old that Daddy died, the child might ask, "Will Daddy be at my birthday party?" and we can begin to explain the concept that death is irreversible and permanent—that people who have died cannot come back to life. When we tell a nine-year-old that her mother died, her question might sound more like "Why did my Mommy have to die?" and we can elaborate on the progressing concepts by explaining that all living things die and oftentimes we cannot predict when death might happen. Six-year-olds are often curious about the physical nature of death and ask questions such as "Can Mommy still play her guitar?" or "Does Daddy still have to shave?" which provides those teachable moments in which we can discuss the concept of nonfunctionality and that dead people no longer breathe, eat, or use a physical body.

Children must have language, examples, and explanations repeated as often as needed. They need the opportunity to practice and repeat language and skills to gain confidence and competency. What is mentionable is manageable. When we help children put words to their thoughts, feelings, and experiences, they are better able to cope. When we provide them with activities and different ways of expressing their internal experience of grief, they are able to put distance between themselves and what is challenging their peace of mind. They have the opportunity to observe, examine, and find solutions from different vantage points through words and activities.

Children Need to See Active, Healthy Models of Grief

Children need role models. They need a hand to hold through the rough terrain of loss and grief. Research suggests that children who have lived through a trauma, such as the death of a parent, are most resilient when they have one healthy adult who tends to their needs. Children need the comfort of knowing that someone more capable and in control has navigated the way ahead of them. Children also need someone to accompany and companion them. Regardless of their age, children need to be shown how to act and express their feelings.

Grieving children need to feel that they have something to contribute and are a valuable part of the family, especially when it is changing, as when a parent or sibling is dying. Often, we do not give children enough credit or give them the opportunity to help, and in that way, we limit their ability to cope. Children can be of service and can learn competency and compassion, building skills for future, inevitable crises. Simple acts of kindness such as making sure the dying family member has water, doing homework next to the bed to keep their loved one company, or reading to the family member are all valuable ways to contribute. We help children become resilient when we keep them close, involved, and informed, especially when we remind them that they are essential parts of the family system.

Characteristics of a Resilient Child

- Has a sense that he has some control, in some way, over his environment

- Has some order and stability in her home life through ritual and routine
- Can let go of inappropriate self-blame and guilt
- Is able to reach out, ask questions, and stay open to receiving help from others
- Is able to identify or have a healthy relationship with at least one helpful adult
- Has a sense of compassion and altruism toward others
- Has a sense of autonomy rather than shame or doubt
- Has a model—either a person or a way of life—that provides guidance as he journeys toward adulthood

Helping Children Become Resilient during Grief

- A grieving child needs just one healthy adult to make a difference. The helper does not need to be the grieving parent.
- Helpers must do their own healthy grief work in order to help a grieving child.
- Modeling coping behaviors shows children *how* to cope. Model coping skills that promote physical health, such as adequate sleep, proper nutrition despite loss of appetite, daily exercise to work out stress, reaching out and accepting emotional support, and expressing grief in your unique way.
- Provide information.
  - ‣ Check for and dispel negative, false myths.
  - ‣ Check for understanding.
  - ‣ Check for meaning.

> Ask: What did he mean to you? What was special about him? What do you miss most about him?

Factors That Increase Risk During Bereavement

Increased risk may include complicated, delayed, prolonged, or exaggerated feelings of grief. The following factors generally predict that a child will have a more difficult time adjusting to a death within the family, particularly of a parent:

- A sudden, unexpected death: There is little or no opportunity for preparation or finishing business.
- Loss of a mother: A mother generally tends more to the rituals and routines of family life that equate to safety, so most children experience more difficulty with the loss of a mother than of a father.
- A lengthy illness: Caregivers may feel depleted and have less time and energy for attending to children's needs.
- Death of another child: A child's death is considered unnatural and untimely. Children exposed to the reality of an early death may lose more of a sense of security if they identify with the deceased child, either through a similarity in age or a meaningful connection.
- A preventable death: Lingering guilt associated with a death that is perceived as preventable inhibits grief resolution.
- Conflict-based relationship: When children's relationship with the deceased was characterized by conflict, the child struggles more with the death.

- Surviving parent liabilities: The functioning level of a surviving parent is the most important predictor for bereaved children's adjustment.
- Inconsistent discipline: Children need routine in the home, especially during times of stress or crisis.
- Parental dating: When a parent dates within the first year after the other parent dies, children's bereavement is intensified. This is especially true when the surviving parent is a father.
- Simultaneous stressors: Children in families with stressors before and after the death have difficulty.
- Nonexpressive grieving styles: Children mimic family members' grieving styles, and passivity does not teach them healthy coping mechanisms.

Notes

1. Centers for Disease Control and Prevention, *Morbidity and Mortality Weekly Report* 59, no. 49 (December 17, 2010), 1609–13.

2. Margaret J. Briggs-Gowan et al., "Prevalence of Exposure to Potentially Traumatic Events in a Healthy Birth Cohort of Very Young Children in the Northeastern United States," *Journal of Traumatic Stress* 23, no. 6 (December 2010), 725–33.

(A helpful internet site to read more about childhood trauma, loss, and treatment can be found at the Child Trauma Institute at www.childtrauma.com/.)

3. Robin F. Goodman, *Caring for Kids after Trauma and Death: A Guide for Parents and Professionals* (New York: The Institute for Trauma and Stress, NYU Child Study Center, 2002).

9

VALIDATION IS THE KEY TO RESOLVING GRIEF

Just having a caring environment in which you can express your feelings and be heard and accepted for who you are is profoundly healing.
JON KABAT-ZINN, *THE POWER OF MEDITATION AND PRAYER*

*R*esolve means "to settle, to work out, or to find meaning." It does not mean to erase or to end, especially when it comes to grief. Grief does not end, but it can be transformed and softened. It can be accepted and can take on another shape rather than taking over a person's life. We can carry grief differently after working through it and finding resolution, but grief does not end. Love for a person does not die just because he did.

All grief needs to be blessed, and in order to be blessed, it must be heard. Someone must be present to our expression of grief, someone who is willing to hold it by listening without judgment or comparison. Our grief, those interior feelings of being deprived of a loved one, is mourned through outward expressions and behaviors. When we wail or tell our story of loss, it is based in the need that our loss not go unnoticed—the death of our loved one will not be overlooked, and our loved one's place in the world will be marked. The story of our personal loss is shared in the world through story, song, art, movement, and ritual so that the deceased is honored. Grief is an expression that validates our loved one's existence in the world and acknowledges that she mattered in our world. Every mourner needs to know that his loved one will be remembered.

Without a safe environment, companionship, and nonjudgmental support, the bereaved tend to metaphorically and physically hold their breath through their grief. As they begin to work through the tasks of grief and realize they can survive, grief may be experienced like coming up from deep in the ocean. The pressure within the body from holding in their grief can burst their mental health and ability to be in the world with others, disorienting them and making them believe they no longer fit in or belong. Unexpressed grief, suffering in silence, or grieving without support can lead to unhealthy stress in the body, which can then lead to more vulnerability and physical illness or depression.

Without the validation that comes from a genuine presence and ability to listen, the bereaved may conclude that their old world is unresponsive, uncaring, and unworthy of their efforts to belong. They experience another loss after the death and feel a sense of disillusionment about whether or not they matter. Bitterness replaces what was once a belief that their community supported them and that they mattered. Without validation and support, mourners can feel disillusioned at the discovery that suffering does not end and that their longed-for happiness will not come.

However, validation can serve as a backboard off of which the bereaved can bounce their thoughts, assumptions, and beliefs and begin to make sense out of their pain, and it has farther reaching effects as well. The act of validation and the skills of empathy and support build a structure within families, communities, and cultures. With this structure, we learn skills and develop compassion for our future challenges and for future generations. We model compassion and patience; we teach our younger generation how to care for the most fragile; and as a community, we begin to build a social fabric that is stronger for practicing these values and practices. We learn that there is value and strength in experiential knowledge. The most valuable aspect of support is the companionship of those who have had personal experience with dying and grief; for example, the Widow-to-Widow support program demonstrates the strength that is realized when widows come together to acknowledge each other's pain and loss.[1] The therapy of choice is peer support.

Validation Is a Concept, a Standard, and an Action

In order to help the bereaved work through their feelings, it is useful to know what validation sounds like and looks like, and how it is experienced. I am often asked the following questions when teaching others how to listen to and validate others:

- What does it sound like to validate and to bless someone's grief? *Validate, support his perspective, and listen between the lines for what is also not said. Listen for the symbolic language and what it means. Ask open-ended questions and clarify what you have heard. And then ask to hear his story again . . . and again.*
- What does it look like to help contain someone else's pain? *Use direct eye contact, appropriate gentle touch, and nodding, and project the energy of leaning into her grief.*
- How will he know that he has been truly heard? *Tell the mourner what you heard him say. Do not try to change, fix, or interpret his feelings or experience. Be present to his truth and what he understands in this moment. Allow and validate his truth and understanding as it evolves and changes.*
- How can I demonstrate that a loved one is important and remembered? *Say the deceased person's name to the mourning person, remember stories that the grieving person has shared, and share your stories of the deceased and how she was meaningful in your life.*

• How do we put standards into practice? *Begin validation now; repeat it often. When in doubt, ask the mourner what would help him feel validated and supported.*

Supporting Those Who Grieve

Those who grieve need verbal and nonverbal permission to feel whatever emotions arise during grief. As a caregiver, tell them and show them that you can be with their pain. Ask them about their loved one, and stay with them as they cry through their story. Their personal way of experiencing their loss should be given consent and validation. The ways they *know* their grief should be honored. Mourners need to be encouraged to express their grief in ways that are most comfortable for them, through words, tears, song, art, movement, or activity. The expression of grief externalizes an internal experience of the loss.

You can help those who grieve by providing emotional, psychological, spiritual, and physical safety to express their grief. This may mean that you maintain confidentiality so they know their grief is safe with you. It means you do not analyze or interpret their feelings without their request. You do not impose your beliefs or agenda upon them but rather serve as a neutral zone where they can explore their feelings and thoughts for as long as necessary. This is especially helpful if a person needs to consider feelings of anger at, or alienation from, God. Safety feels like a soft place where they can land during the darkest night of their anguish.

While grieving, those in pain need a sense of a compassionate presence. That comes in the form of a person who provides a sense of safety and a healthy relationship, and companions them. It is the person who can just be with them in whatever way is helpful throughout the journey. There may be several people who can offer support with their ability to be present, and each may provide different aspects that are needed. Dr. Therese Rando, the clinical director of the Institute for the

Study and Treatment of Loss, conceptualized five needs of the
bereaved.[2]

The Five Needs of the Bereaved

1. *To Be Cared For.* The bereaved need to be cared for emotionally,
   physically, and spiritually. The bereaved know when we come with
   that ability; it is apparent in our attitude and attention of care. You
   can feel more confident that you are bringing the commitment of
   service to a mourner if you practice the **five Ps**:
   - **Presence** refers to your commitment to be there for the mourner
     through the struggle with his thoughts, feelings, and memories
     that may have frightened others away. (Grief can bring up anger as
     well as sadness.) Your presence is far more important than your
     knowledge or advice; what is most needed is your acknowledgment
     of his pain and sorrow.
   - **Permission** describes the attitude you bring. It is felt when you are
     open, interested, and nonjudgmental as the mourner shares infor-
     mation, feelings, and memories. Permission avoids speaking of
     what one should do or should feel. It recognizes that each person
     feels and processes grief in unique ways.
   - **Patience** refers to your attitude of putting into practice the recog-
     nition that grief is painful, difficult, and often slow. It refers to the
     practice of being in the present, moment after moment, with open-
     ness to what is. Patience is helpful in order to hear the same story
     many times without reminding the mourner that you have already
     heard it. Remember that "every loss deserves a hundred tellings."[3]
   - **Predictability** encompasses your dependability, consistency, and
     trustworthiness, allowing the mourner to feel the security of know-
     ing you will act to protect her and the memory of her loved one.
   - **Perseverance** is the quality of enduring throughout a process that
     can be long, painful, and frustrating at times. It implies that you

will remain with the bereaved whenever you can, and you will be honest when you have limitations or boundaries. It implies going the distance while also being aware of healthy boundaries and realistic limitations, with the goal of being a companion through the dark nights of the soul.

2. *To Have Their Feelings Acknowledged and the Loved One Remembered.* When in doubt about how to help, keep in mind the importance of acknowledging and remembering. Perhaps the greatest comfort we can offer is remembrance. Listen to the stories, share vignettes, and help the mourner review his memories. Stories add a dimension to the recollections and expand the wealth of memories of his loved one. Stories are a way of knowing that the deceased was an important part of the world and will not be forgotten. A story is a specific example of how and why a person will be remembered. Stories help the bereaved to make sense of events and build meaning out of loss.

3. *To Have Their Feelings and Needs Normalized.* There are many ways to communicate that grief is normal and to encourage its expression. We help a mourner when we tell her or show her that her grief is unique and deserves its personal expression.

   • We normalize grief when we can expect and lessen the mourner's anxiety about the multitude of emotions within grief. We can explain and allow for the numbness of grief. We can help him tolerate the physical and emotional exhaustion of grief. We can respond to the wave of grief attacks that occur when he does not expect it.

   • We help when we support her requests for help. And if we know we are unable to be that resource to provide the help, we can encourage her to use other support systems and help her to find the resources she needs.

- We can encourage and participate in personal, meaningful rituals surrounding death. We may also participate in rituals on the anniversary of the loss, years afterward, when the mourner continues to feel the grief but also feels that he remembers alone.

4. **To Be Heard.** When I worked as a volunteer hospital chaplain, I thought of myself as a professional listener. Listening is a ministry. Although it appears to be a passive act—many may not understand the act of listening as doing for another person—when I listen, much more is involved than just my ears. To truly listen is to engage your ears, eyes, heart, and intuition. To listen is to open so fully to another person as to take her story into yourself and digest it on every level.

- When I listen deeply to another, it is as though all my senses and attention surround and hold the speaker and his story. Listening is the art of experiencing what the world is like for the person talking. It is a surrender of assumptions and prejudices, and a surrender of walls so that you might accept how it is to be that other person. Acceptance is a form of validation and does not require that you understand but rather that you make room for the mourner's experience.

- When we validate, we are expressing that there is someone else in the world who has shared a similar feeling or experience. A mourner works with a counselor so that she might be heard, and have her story acknowledged. She can receive validation for her perspective, have a companion in her pain, and be assured that her feelings are real and that she is not crazy. She needs to be held, and listening is perhaps the best vehicle for that holding.

- Listening with the heart does not ask that you do it *right*, but only that you do it with *attention* and *intention*. If listening is genuine, healing takes place. You hold the energy of curiosity, confusion, joy, pain, or questions until the speaker feels safe and heard. You acknowledge the world of the speaker. It is as though a soothing mantra echoes in the rooms of his heart: "I am seen, and I am known." You do not actually create healing, but the act of genuine listening opens the speaker to his own healing potential. To be heard, seen, and known is to heal the spiritual disconnections, physical discomforts, and intellectual confusions.

- Listening is a ministry. It is an act of holding another and acknowledging her story as real and sacred. Listening is also a discipline. I use the disciple's stance that asks of me nothing more than remembering who I am, where I come from, and that I am a reflection of a power greater than myself. I am connected to all sentient beings. I am here to love. Remembering that, it is a simple task to reflect love and to let the image of a great listener wash over me.

- I am listening well when I experience a significant level of intimacy with another person. In that moment of deep listening, I see a beautiful golden aura that envelops both of us. Its sparkling ring of light around the two of us makes me feel that we are no longer separate beings—we are connected on an emotional and spiritual level. Perhaps it is the loss of attention to my body and its little discomforts that so often get in the way of being fully present with another person. I have stopped giving room to those distractions that take my focus from another person. The chatter in my mind ceases and my senses are sharper, as if my body were at once one big ear, one big eye, and one fine-tuned radar of intuition.

- This intimacy is a *way of being* so that the other person reports feeling seen, heard, and acknowledged from a soul level. It is similar to waking from a profound dream state, unable to remember the details of the dream. It is an experience known as state-bound consciousness. If you can disengage from the struggle of remembering, you can trust that a level of healing occurred, and you both have been touched at a deep and profound level.

- Listening is a spiritual practice. Listening is a prayer. As a listener, I must be still, serene, and accepting. When I am still and receptive in the act of listening, it is as though I am inviting the speaker to see herself clearly reflected in a still lake. The placid water accurately mirrors the image presented. If there were ripples from the listener's reaction or defensiveness, the image would be distorted. If you as the listener offer anything less than full attention, your reaction creates its own agitation superimposed over the original soul material, and that is a disservice to the speaker. Real listening is being that still lake, reflecting the original. It requires a faith in the other person, believing that there is a divinity and a wealth of resources within that person. They do not need to be fixed or corrected or educated. The gift that is called for is listening. In the deep calm of the act of listening, people tell me they feel healed.

5. **To Be Seen and Acknowledged.** It is extremely helpful to feel seen, or as one mourner said, "When I am with you, I feel *felt*." A person going through profound grief, needing a sense of security, safety, and hope for the future, finds those needs fulfilled largely in the emotional quality of connections with caring others. You can provide this by accompanying the mourner deeply and often as he expresses a wide range of feelings. The quality that heals comes from creating and protecting a safe environment—without distractions or interruptions, without judgment or analysis—that diverts the mourner from the pain he is trying to understand.

- To deny, ignore, or minimize one's grief exacerbates her pain. It turns pain into suffering. It does not make the grief go away but instead prolongs and deepens the distress of loss. By engaging in the work of grief, we move through loss, face the fears and obstacles, moving in the direction of renewal, and begin again to engage in our future.

We Validate When We Hold Another Person's Pain

I was privileged to be with Carla, a woman dying of leukemia whose bone marrow transplant had been unsuccessful. More painful than the weeks in the isolation unit, losing her hair, and the transplant itself was her desperate struggle to be loved by her broken family. Throughout her short life, she had been abandoned by an alcoholic mother, abused by an angry father, and humiliated by grandparents. In her last months, knowing that the transplant was unsuccessful and the leukemia was continuing to feed on her body, she fought her hardest battle to make peace with her family and ask for what she needed.

Carla's father responded by traveling to the cancer center to be with her for her transplant. But, she said, he was only with her physically, and she felt the old sting of separation and alienation from the man she most wanted to love her. Gradually, her determination and fight soured into anger and resentment. She looked like a red, roaring flame of rage, and her tone of voice hissed like a coiled snake. The nursing staff confronted her, avoided her, and told me they felt drained after working with her. Carla told me she wanted to shrivel up and die.

Between her words, I heard her grief, frustration, and longing. She had worked so fiercely to build up hope and to share love, but she now believed that she had used it all up. All that was left was the anger, and that was devouring all the light within her. I held out my cupped hands and asked her if she would allow me to keep her hope and her love for her in a safe place. "I will keep it in a chamber of my heart, under lock and key," I told her. I would guard and nurture those energies, and she could have the hope and love back whenever she felt strong enough again to carry them herself. The hope and love were hers—I was merely holding her potential for healing because, I told her, I believed in her timing, her process, and her own resources. She needed a guardian for her struggle, someone who would champion and encourage her when she felt like giving up but wanted to go on. Carla needed an external mirror to remind her that she had once experienced love and healing, and she could again. She needed permission to feel disappointed. She needed a way to allow the energy of anger and resentment to spend itself without adding to her *dis-ease*.

It was a simple act of symbolic *holding* that I performed. Sometimes it is just a part of a person that needs to be held, cradled, comforted, and protected. In Carla's case, it was her healthy, hopeful, loving self that needed a safe space. I created a visual image by cupping my hands, showing Carla where she could lay her hope and love, like a wounded child into a caregiver's arms.

Weeks later Carla told me she felt she had made peace and that she felt strong enough to take back her hope and love. She told me that I had shown her a way to accept all the parts of herself because I was willing to acknowledge and validate her rage. Once validated rather than judged, she could spend time trying to understand and work with her feelings. She did not feel that she could have attended to the work of understanding her rage if she had been worried about what she called the good parts of her—the hope and love—being harmed.

Carla died soon afterward. When I think of Carla now, I remember a snapshot of time as I held my cupped hands toward her and she put both her hands in mine. That moment was an act of faith in her own powers of resolution and healing, and in my ability to nurture and safeguard a precious part of her. And in the next instant, I remember the moment when she asked for her hope and love back, and the courage that it must have taken to believe in and act from a position of peace. That moment of peace was also her moment of healing.

We Can Heal Grief Over Time and with Work

There are signs, differences in your reactions, that indicate that you are working through your grief. These are important signals that you are not stuck and that your grief is changing.

- When you can see the whole picture of your deceased loved one and review both the happy and the unhappy memories of your life together, you are moving into a realistic understanding of the person and your relationship.
- You can trust that you are healing when you do not take the comments, suggestions, or evaluations of others personally, and you understand that they are made out of ignorance or a lack of experience.
- When you notice that your physical health and energy have improved and your appetite, sleep patterns, and exercise drive are closer to what they were before the death, then you can take comfort in your movement toward healing. When you are not exhausted, you can concentrate on reading or a task, and you have energy when you wake in the morning, you can be reassured that your grief is abating.
- Moving on does not mean you are leaving behind the good memories or meanings—there are more good times now when you can enjoy time alone, establish and enjoy new relationships, and accept things as they are and not spend the majority of your time returning to the past. When you no longer feel you have to make weekly trips to the cemetery, you have time to develop new, good experiences.
- Your grief has changed and your pain has strengthened you when you feel confident again; you choose to reach out to help someone else who has experienced a similar loss, and you can organize and plan for a future with meaning and purpose.
- Your grief is healing when you find yourself listening to the music you associate with your loved one and you smile in gratitude rather than cry in pain. When you can laugh and enjoy a joke without feeling guilty, feel grateful and recognize the beauty around you again, look forward to holidays and participate in social gatherings, and have patience with yourself and with others, you can claim that your healing has taken residence where the grief was.

Rituals Validate Grief and the
Change in Our Lives

Rituals can include any external sign, symbol, or activity that mirrors what the social group has experienced, believes, and values. The ritual, whether it is formal or informal, religious or secular, marks a person or group's change in life. In the last century, the symbol of a black armband informed a community that its wearer was grieving the loss of a loved one; it served as an invitation for condolences and a reminder to be accommodating toward the bereaved. A black wreath on a front door also served as an external sign of the internal process of mourning. When a family gathers around a gravesite and feasts together, laying offerings at the grave for the deceased, it is a ritual to remember and include their deceased loved one and reflects their beliefs of a continuing relationship.

Rituals are helpful because they bring attention to the fact that there has been a significant change to the life of the community. Ritual is a tangible way to honor the deceased, as well as the surviving loved ones and the community that are affected. Rituals bring people together to acknowledge and validate the relationship between the deceased and the survivors, and to honor the place of the deceased in the community's collective life. Rituals may also serve to express or demonstrate the deceased person's legacy and their ongoing contribution to an individual or a community.

Ritual offers an occasion to reassure and reestablish social connection and cohesion. It can reintegrate a family's solidarity and reestablish morale, especially after a traumatic death such as a suicide or murder. Rituals strengthen the bonds and sense of purpose within a family, and they also serve to confirm our bonds with people and life experiences beyond this moment. Depending on people's spiritual beliefs and needs, rituals can create order by connecting the deceased to ancient relatives, and they can communicate purpose or meaning in suffering.

❧ ❧ ❧

How to Create a Ritual

- Perform a ritual of reconciliation. Create a visualization or guided meditation and imagine communicating with the deceased. Request and offer forgiveness for any acts that were left unaddressed before death.
- Create an empty chair exercise. Set two chairs facing each other. Sit in one chair and talk to your loved one in the empty chair about whatever it is you need to share. Switch chairs and imagine being your deceased loved one, speaking for her in response to your sharing. Continue the dialogue, switching chairs and taking on her role as you complete the communication.
- Write a letter to the deceased. Bury it, burn it, or save it in a special box depending on the purpose and content.
- Make a memory book. Arrange photographs and memorabilia of your loved one in one book or a special box.
- Plant a tree or designate a special place to relax and be with the memories of the deceased.
- Spend time in your loved one's favorite space. Sit in his favorite chair or visit the park he enjoyed walking in.
- Light a candle on a regular basis or to mark any anniversary of meaning.

Create, or design and commission, a memory quilt. The quilt honors the significant life events of your loved one.

❧ ❧ ❧

Disenfranchised Grief Exacerbates and Delays Normal Grief

Disenfranchised grief is what people experience when they incur a loss that is not—or cannot be—openly acknowledged, socially sanctioned, or publicly mourned. The rights and rituals that are usually extended to mourners are typically not offered if the deceased was considered socially invisible—a person who is less valued in some cultures, such as the institutionalized person, the drug addict, the homeless, the stillborn child, the miscarried fetus, or the suicidal. Normal grieving compassion is often not offered to those grieving the socially dead, those people who may be present in body but not fully functioning, such as Alzheimer's or comatose patients. In these cases, the bereaved may not be offered the rights or status of the grieving role, and they have more difficulty receiving social support, sympathy, or compensation. Their grief is done in private and with few resources.

Disenfranchised mourners may be excluded from caring for the dying or from funeral rituals, which may lead to feelings of guilt, anger, and unresolved grief. Resolution to this additional layer of grief comes by finding support, making the grief visible, finding someone to whom they can talk out their grief, and creating meaningful rituals.

For mourners experiencing this divide, reaching out for help is the first step. Clarifying and understanding a disenfranchised mourner's grief as real, significant, and valid is important, but he also needs social validation. That grief needs to find ways to be expressed in the world. Grief needs to be shared in words and rituals, honored with others in the community, and reviewed as often as the mourner feels necessary. To grieve alone, because society judges a person's loss, may make her feel like she is grieving in shame.

⋙ ⋙ ⋙

Ways to Validate Death

- Share a personal memory of the deceased.
- If you did not know the deceased well enough to have a memory to share, ask your grieving friend to share a remembrance with you.
- Give your undivided listening attention ... and then listen more.
- Run errands or provide groceries.
- Do the yard work the day before the family is gathering at the house for the service.
- Remember the death after a month, six months, and a year with a card, a memory, and a visit.

If ...

- If we allow that grief is different for each mourner, then we allow for differences and judge less.
- If we know that grief can be untimely and exhausting, then we are less anxious when our body speaks our grief through physical symptoms (chest pains, aches, tight throat).
- If we know that grief is expressed emotionally and spiritually, then we allow and learn from what is expressed in those dimensions, accelerating our recovery.
- If we judge and compare others less, then we can be present for greater service.

Notes

1. Phyllis R. Silverman, *Widow to Widow: How the Bereaved Help One Another* (New York: Routledge, 2004).

2. Therese A. Rando, PhD, *Treatment of Complicated Mourning* (Champaign, IL: Research Press, 1993).

3. Hospice of the Monterey Peninsula, "Good Grief," Griefbusters program (Monterey, CA: Community Hospital of the Monterey Peninsula, 1985).

10

WE CAN FIND MEANING
IN LOSS

*There are two ways to live your life—one is as though nothing is a miracle,
the other is as though everything is a miracle.*

ALBERT EINSTEIN

I feel grateful that I became conscious of misfortune at an early age. I am no different than others who have encountered tragedy and heartache; my good fortune was that I became aware and made a decision to make meaning of my mother's death. I changed the way I thought about her death, and because of that decision, I changed my pain. I put the pain into action, and I changed any drama into purpose. I found significance in her death, which has given my life direction and purpose.

For my own survival, I had to make sense of and create order out of the chaos of the death of a young woman, a mother to three children. Her death felt like total anarchy of any order that I needed as a thirteen-year-old. To avoid spinning out of control, I told myself that I would make her death matter. I filled the sudden, unexpected void with value. I used her death as a vehicle to move forward, rather than a weight to collapse under in despair. I reasoned that anger and self-pity would negate the essence of her.

I did not find any meaning to her death immediately. I had to wrestle through many dark nights of the soul and embrace all of my feelings.

I discovered meaning from different perspectives and in different cultures; I traveled abroad and learned from others how they grieved and how they made sense of death. I wrote in a journal to externalize my feelings so I could see my confusion penned out in front of me. I needed to find someone to listen to my stories, over and over. I had to be with my grief if I was going to release it.

Eventually I found a way to transform my grief through acceptance and gratitude. When I changed my perspective and understood her death from another point of view, my grief gave me purpose and a reason for being. What I wanted to do with my life became more powerful—and more absorbing—than the pain I felt about my mother's death.

My life became about validating and listening to others' pain. Some of those people were dying and some were the loved ones left behind. In the end, my mother's death became the chisel with which I sculpted my life. In finding meaning in her death, I found a way of being in the world. Discovering meaning meant that her death was not wasted; she did not die in vain.

Many have endured the journey of loss and discovery and have had to dig deeper to find the courage to forgive, find meaning, and move forward. Victor Frankl, renowned twentieth-century Austrian neurologist and psychologist, lost everything in a Nazi concentration camp during World War II. His father, mother, brother, and wife were killed. He suffered through hunger, brutality, and the theft of his every possession. Despite this overwhelming degradation engulfed in profound fear and loss, Frankl was able to find his will to live by retaining memories of his loved ones, a faith in something greater than himself, a sense of humor, and gratitude in the healing beauty of nature. He actively pursued meaning and purpose in his suffering, and he chronicled his experiences in the profound book *Man's Search for Meaning*. His survival and ultimate freedom came from rising above his external circumstances and choosing his attitude and perspective.

You Are the Expert on Your Experience and Loss

It is your story. You write and live your story through your attitudes, expectations, and beliefs about the world. Your story's most powerful impact comes not from the black-and-white facts but rather from your interpretations and attitudes about this specific loss. The power to heal is a result of what you have learned from all your personal losses and the losses of others. The conditions surrounding the death of a loved one may appear to be objective and real, but there is a subtler force that has a greater impact on the quality of your life. It is your personal decision about what you want to see and experience in life that creates the quality of your life. It is your greatest power to decide what and how you experience your life, and it depends not on what happens to you, but on how you decide to attribute meaning to any event.

We all have choices; those choices are within ourselves. Those choices are responses and reactions to what is, to what happens outside of each of us. Loss and death, pain and grief can be corrosive forces to a human being and a family, or they can be an opening and opportunity for growth and strength. As David Harkins writes,

> You can shed tears that she is gone,
> or you can smile because she has lived.
> You can close your eyes and pray that she'll come back,
> or you can open your eyes and see all she's left.
> Your heart can be empty because you can't see her,
> or you can be full of the love you shared.[1]

Your ability to accept and find meaning can heal your reality and the quality of your life.

"Dad had lung cancer. I dropped everything in my life to be with him, thinking that we had months to be together; we had only twelve days after I arrived." These are facts. But they do not tell the whole story, and they do not show the freedom of choice that my father claimed. The facts do not illustrate the sense of peace I derived from finding meaning. The facts could have reflected only the physical pain of illness and the sadness of a future without him. Or the story could include the moments during those thirteen days when we laughed, reviewed memories and photos, and thanked each other in a hundred ways. There were choices, and in the end, I chose to make those that left me with gratitude, peace, and meaning.

The power of my choices showed me that we captured a whole lifetime in those mere thirteen days. To sustain myself through his pain and my grief, I played a game in which I searched for the gifts in each day and shared them aloud as I tucked my father into bed. We focused on the joys of the day together rather than on his struggle to breathe. This is not to suggest that we ignored those times of his physical or emotional distress; he brought them to my attention or I noticed, and we responded to whatever need arose in the moment. But that was not the focus of our time together. His cancer, his struggle, and his death would not be what I remembered at the end of his life.

We can choose to see a loved one's illness and death as a doorway through which we both passed, and we become changed forever. We can learn something from loss. We can find gifts in the challenge and the pain. But first, we must choose that perspective and move toward that choice. Then we begin the work of making meaning.

How We Make Meaning from Loss

How we make meaning is a choice. It consists of creating our place in the world and finding purpose in our life story. It is like a fairy tale that gives structure and meaning to a life, like the bones that hold us up in our crises and through our challenges. The meaning, or story of a life, helps us make sense of it. We can deal with negative events by changing our life perspective so that it includes understanding and acceptance.

We can change our perception of the event, transition from blame to acceptance, once we have compassion. When we expand our ability to validate life in spite of death, we change our attitude about the past. We change our perception of death from an absolute evil or obliteration to a significant event that can give life meaning. In order to find meaning, we ask questions such as *What can I learn from this?* and *Where is the gift in this?* instead of stating absolutes.

When a lung cancer patient cannot fill his lungs with air, he might sigh heavily and often in order to try to replenish his oxygen and self-soothe. He might feel frustrated and fearful, thinking, *I can't get enough air.* However, that same person might shift his awareness, feel whatever air he is able to hold as a gift, and hear himself sighing. He becomes aware that his sighing sounds like waves lapping on his favorite beach, and he no longer resists his experience but instead enters it with a greater appreciation and acceptance. His new perspective and the ability to pay attention open him to possibilities that lead to a softer, more compassionate experience of what is.

The qualities of trust, listening, and attention to the changing experiences of death and loss are what change the experience from negativity to possibility. The journey becomes more of a fearless adventure. It is not easy, nor does everything encountered feel good, but by being open and receptive to the situation as it is, the circumstance loses its edge of fear, anger, and unnecessary pain. The Zen teacher Shunryu Suzuki Roshi writes in *Zen Mind, Beginner's Mind,* "In the beginner's mind, there are many possibilities, but in the expert's there are few."

When we can *just* observe, we are able to see the experience without judging or attaching our needs to whatever is happening. We can observe our emotions and watch without criticism as we judge ourselves less. We have more compassion and patience for our feelings and our journey, and we feel less alone. Through it all, if we can stay open without judgment, we can see and experience more perspectives, more options, and greater meaning. If we can attend to our dying loved one with a beginner's mind, without judgment, there are more paths to take because there are more possibilities.

We begin to feel the healing of our grief when we accept that the event of our loved one's death is in the past. We do not relive the time of death with the same physical sensations; we do not hold our breath as we tell the story or sob without being able to talk. Now, as we heal, it is as though we are sitting in a theater and observing a movie. We have a physical and emotional distance to the picture we are seeing in our mind's eye. We know that the events are not happening in this present time and that we are not in the story in the same way.

It is not simply time but also insight into the meaning of death that lead to our ability to cope. The more we heal, the more we are able to remember the death of our loved one—even the most disturbing incidents surrounding the death—as a memory with appropriate sadness, but not as though we are reliving the experience with the same intensity of physical and emotional sensation. The anguish and accompanying emotions of anxiety, fear, anger, and despair feel farther away. We can tell the story and recall every detail of the death but without feeling overwhelmed and overcome.

When we can recall a loved one's death as though we are observing a movie and recognize our self as a character in the story, when we are able to just observe and discover parts of the story that we did not fully understand before, when we can watch the journey unfold and not feel that it is a judgment against us, then we are beginning to heal. True healing understands that the story of loss has been told millions of times, in hundreds of languages, and that we are not alone.

Our anguish softens when we recognize that death is inevitable and is an event that is shared with all other human beings. We begin to heal when we accept that our loved one's life is over but ours is not, and when we recognize that the distinction is neither an act of disloyalty nor a sign of not loving enough. How we grieve has nothing to do with how well we loved. A mother who used to blame herself for not knowing more (than even the doctors) about her son's disease realizes that "I should have known more" is not a realistic expectation and was not possible at the time. Her strong self-condemnation lightens into "I wish I could have," and she understands that her self-reproach came from a place of wanting more control than she could possibly have had.

The physical separation from the death of a loved one is a palpable pain held in the body. The emotional pain we as survivors feel is a reflection of what the death means about the deceased, us, and our relationship. In other words, at the death of a child, a parent often thinks, *I am a bad parent* or *I am not good enough*. Those thoughts are often unconscious, but they may drive us toward self-reproach and punishment for the rest of our lives if they are not uncovered and brought to awareness. Sharing our pain with others reveals the common ground most of us have experienced. We are not alone. Death and separation happen to everyone. We can stop labeling ourselves as bad, not good enough, victims, or abandoned. We can work to accept our limitations, lack of control, and limited resources. We can accept our humanity.

There are insights that can help us cope. We each have a different story, perhaps with a different context, but grief is universal. We *all* experience the death of a family member. We *all* lose a loved one. It is helpful and comforting to remember that we are not singled out. We are not victims. This death is not a personal punishment against you. Death is universal. It did not happen just to you.

We make meaning in order to change our understanding of what has happened, the legacy of one's life, and what is now possible for us going forward. It is not *what* happened to us that matters but *how* we come to make sense of what happened that predicts our emotional health and future. We tell stories to bring what is inside of us to the outside, so that we understand the meaning of events. In this way, telling the story of our loss over and over is how we create a more positive, healthy understanding from a potential tragedy. If we can make sense of our pain, we can change.

We make meaning in order to construct how we will remember our loved one and how we will remember our relationship with that person. We make meaning to change the events that are remembered, how they are remembered, and with what or whom those memories will be associated. The meanings we attach to the event of the illness, dying process, or dying moment will color how we live in the world now and in the future.

As caregivers, we can help mourners by encouraging them to tell their story over and over. Every time a memory is reviewed, the intensity of suffering has the potential to be softened. Recent research suggests that memory is "plastic" and that each time we bring a memory to mind we may alter it in some way.[2] Our story may change over time as our understanding changes. How we perceive the events, understand the context and the connections, and articulate the narrative can change over time, with review. Research and interventions used in therapeutic settings for post-traumatic stress disorder show that exposing and recalling traumatic events, such as the death of a loved one, do not erase a memory but can change the quality of the memory. The feelings of distress become weaker and have less of a negative impact on the survivor. Telling our story and finding meaning keeps us from living in the past.

What Is Mentionable Becomes Manageable

We need to give our sorrow words. Stories bring the internal experience out into the external world so that we can share it with others. When we share and connect, we build a network of support to which we can go for validation and resources. As important as the *event* is, the *meaning* and *how we come to make sense of it* are even more important. When we are able to find meaning in the event, we feel less disorganized. When we make the story more coherent, we begin to understand the larger picture. We find that our world is not all about loss, but it is also about beauty and blessings within the pain. In the end, we emerge with hope and our wholeness intact.

Instead of battling grief, we are strong enough to engage in a deeper exploration of what is, to be so courageous as to mingle with grief in order to find the meaning and gift in it. The closer we examine it, the more intimate it becomes, the more it is our own, and the less ambiguous and vague. We can hold it rather than it taking hold of us. We can know it so that it can inform us of what is most precious to us.

In the exploration, we learn that not only can we tolerate our pain but we can also transcend it, and see it for what it is and what it is not. It is *only* pain; it is not more powerful than love. It is a reaction to the illusion that love is lost. When we realize that we are holding the memory of our loved one so close that we have memorized the texture of her skin and we can draw the contour of her face or recite her favorite stories and we know how she would respond to a question, we know without hesitation that her essence is present. We know that joy and sorrow, love and grief can coexist.

Death Does Not End a Relationship

As we have shared life with a loved one in the physical world, after his death we must learn to carry that loved one in a new way. I am still a daughter, though my parents are dead. The word *daughter* can be both a noun and a verb. I decided to continue to daughter, to be an active representation of my father in the world. I care for his friends in ways that I know he would appreciate, I support causes that continue his legacy, and I live the values that he taught me. I express myself as a daughter, and I continue to daughter.

Dr. Robert Lifton wrote about a "symbolic immortality" as we learn to live and acknowledge the values, meanings, and legacy left to us by the deceased.[3] We can make our focus the mystery of the immortal aspects of our loved one's life. Our opportunity is to retain and cherish what we have been given from our loved one and the relationship. We can choose to take that and shape our future years, weaving that legacy into our new life.

Old homes and neighborhoods we shared with our loved one hold reminders, memories, and benchmarks of our life together and so hold parts of our loved one. Sometimes we believe that if we leave the home we made together, we will leave the love behind, as though walls could confine love. Likewise we hang on tenaciously to our grief in a mistaken, ritualistic way of holding on to love. But I would suggest that those things, places, and people that remind us of our loved one serve as a backboard from which the love comes back to us. I believe we can carry that backboard with us into a new place because it is really our mind and our heart that hold our loved one and our history together.

We can expand our resources and the things that will evoke our loved one for us by:

1. Making a list of the things in the home that will remind us of him

2. Creating anniversaries that celebrate our history together

3. Continuing to relate to our loved one and share who we are becoming

4. Sharing stories of our loved one with new friends as we would share stories of our history

In essence, we can learn a different form of attachment and ways of belonging to our loved one. We can carry our loved one with us rather than leave him behind.

Death ends a physical life but not our emotional connection to our loved one. Death changes the nature of the relationship, but it does not sever our continuing bond of love. Our fear of death says, "You are alone, and you have lost the battle for life," but when we remember the strength of our love and connection, we hear the truth from within and around us echoing, "I am always with you."

Years of research and thousands of reports confirm that close to 50 percent of adults have felt contact from someone who has died. Researchers estimate that fifty to one hundred million Americans have had a contact experience, or after-death communication, which includes:[4]

- Intuitive: sensing a presence or an internal knowing
- Auditory: laughter, voice, breath, or favorite music identified with the deceased
- Tactile: a touch, embrace, or physical presence
- Smell: the scent of something the deceased wore or the aroma of something associated with the deceased, such as bath powder or tobacco
- Signs or symbols: meaningful objects associated with the deceased
- Dreams: information or comfort received in a particularly vivid way that has a different quality from normal dreams

The increasing number of reports and attention from research on after-death communication offers a sense of normalcy to the thousands of mourners who have these kinds of experiences after the death of a loved one. These contact experiences can bring comfort, solace, and often reconciliation to questions and anxiety about death. A communication from a deceased loved one usually comes with the message "I am okay" or "I love you," and brings an awareness that the relationship is continuing on in a different form.

My father's presence comforted me on the first anniversary of his death and reinforced what hundreds of grieving loved ones have told me: consciousness, relationships, and love continue after death. Parents of a six-month-old boy who died suddenly and unexpectedly of sudden infant death syndrome (SIDS) told me of their experience of waking at the same time to discover that they had shared the same profound visitation from their deceased son—the child, without the ability to speak, had come to them in a dream, and both his mother and father received the same message: "I'm okay, and I am always with you." The gift of these kinds of communications dispels fears and provides hope that the power of love is stronger than death.

In my work with grieving parents of a deceased child, I routinely ask them if they have had any form of communication from their child. These parents consistently share a sigh of relief that someone has openly inquired about such a significant event. They go on to recount a story oft told by others. When I validate their experience and share the research findings that thousands of others report similar experiences, they sometimes tell me that their after-death communication was the single greatest gift of peace they could have received after such a tragedy. Having others openly inquire, accept, and validate such a gift strengthens their conviction that the relationship and bond continue, despite death.

NOTES

1. This poem, "She Is Gone," was found and used by Queen Elizabeth at the funeral of her mother, the Queen Mother, in April 2002. The author is David Harkins, a former baker and current painter, from Cumbria, who wrote the piece in the early 1980s as an homage to an unrequited love (http://www.poeticexpressions.co.uk/POEMS/You%20can%20shed%20tears%20that%20she%20is%20gone.htm).

2. "Plastic Brain Outsmarts Experts: Training Can Increase Fluid Intelligence, Once Thought To Be Fixed At Birth," *Science Daily* (June 5, 2008).

3. According to Dr. Robert J. Lifton, healthy individuals seek a sense of life continuity, or immortality, through symbolic means. Dr. Lifton coined the concept "symbolic immortality" to refer to the universal human quest to achieve a sense of continuity in the face of the incontrovertible evidence that we will die. According to Dr. Lifton, the knowledge that we will die forces us to confront and transcend our fears of finitude in symbolic ways, which connect us to the past and present, linking us to

those who have gone before us and to those who will live on after us and remember our contributions.

Robert J. Lifton, *The Broken Connection: On Death and the Continuity of Life* (Washington, DC: American Psychiatric Press, Inc., 1979).

Dr. Lifton proposes five modes of symbolic connectedness or immortality, which he identifies as (1) biological, (2) creative, (3) transcendental, (4) natural, and (5) experiential transcendence.

Robert J. Lifton, "The Sense of Immortality: On Death and the Continuity of Life," *American Journal of Psychoanalysis* 33 (1973), 3–15.

4. Maggie Callanan and Patricia Kelley, *Final Gifts: Understanding the Special Awareness, Needs, and Communications of the Dying* (New York: Bantam, 1993).

In this book the authors note several recurring themes from over two hundred patients, the main one being that the dying person often felt accompanied by another person who had already died. The significant message from these communications was that the dying person was not alone.

Bill and Judy Guggenheim, *Hello from Heaven!* (New York: Bantam, 2005).

CONCLUSION

Someone once wrote that how we handle our deepest wounds is the equivalent of how we will approach our dying. We can accept our death and the death of a loved one by searching for growth, meaning, and transformation; or we can recoil, deny, and become angry about the inevitable, thereby missing the opportunity to stretch into our greatest potential. It is a choice. You can make life and death less difficult, more peaceful. You can find the peace now by seeking meaning and using it in your life.

We can and must learn to live with death, dying, and grief so that we can live without fear. When fear is not the compass with which we navigate life, we do not miss opportunities to be present to all of life, the challenges as well as the joys. It is then, when we have overcome fear, that we live a more self-determined life full of personal choice that reflects our most authentic self. When we can make choices out of love and acceptance rather than fear and avoidance, we can live right up to the moment of our death or remain present for the death of our loved one. We live fully, we connect fully, and we die knowing we took our own authentic path.

It took my mother's death to unveil my purpose and potential. I had to make the decision and choice to discover the meaning and the gifts in her death and my grief. I spent my life learning the skills, developing a competency with death, and practicing confidence with dying patients in order to do for my father what I could not do for my mother. I wish I had known these things before my mother died, but I hope my experiences with death, dying, and grief will set you on a journey that makes a difference.

We can develop and strengthen bonds of love that continue after death through service to one another. Even in the midst of decline, illness, and the prognosis of imminent death, we can build trust, we can care and be cared for, and we can share vulnerabilities. Even in the midst of great sadness, we can build and maintain the connections we cherish most. We can support our loved one's life and according to his unique and authentic values. We all will die, and we may not change the timing or the cause of death, but we can make a difference in the process. We can make choices that change how illness and dying are experienced by the dying and the family. Our choices can be life affirming and relationship enhancing rather than death avoidant and isolating. We can become familiar and competent with death so we practice life to its fullest.

We have a responsibility to ourselves, to our loved ones, and to the next generation to care. We are wired to care. Caring is like the synapses between nerves; caring connects one generation to another and transmits the electric impulses of our humanity. Caring is in our DNA in order to survive and thrive. We care best when we accept what is and push nothing away, when we offer our whole self to whatever is going on, when we put aside our agenda and accept our loved one's choices, and when we respond now instead of waiting until it is too late. Caring for our dying loved one is an opportunity of a lifetime, a sacred gift of trust both given and received.

PART III

RECOMMENDED
RESOURCES

APPENDIX A

LETTERS ON DEATH AND DYING

B efore now, you may not have had an experience with someone who was dying. Dying is unique to each individual, and even if you have assisted many through an illness and their dying, the person you are caring for now has different needs, values, and challenges. It is not necessarily an obstacle if you are new to these demands and challenges because to come without assumptions, comparisons, or your own agenda is a powerful and helpful position from which to serve. The following are common letters I receive from families I have worked with and counseled, and from those seeking help through a national website of bereaved family members to whom I respond.

Pre-Death Visions Comfort the Dying

Dear Dr. Leary:

My brother said he saw his best friend who died before him, and I don't know how to respond. Is he hallucinating?

—John

Dear John:

Many people who are nearing death report that they see, hear, or feel friends or loved ones who have died before them. Some describe individuals whom they had never met before, and family members can identify them as deceased family members. These experiences most often comfort, rather than scare, the dying person because of the feelings that they evoke and the message that is conveyed by the deceased loved ones. These kinds of experiences also lead many people to believe in the survival of consciousness and the continuing bond of love.

You can support your brother by asking him open-ended questions that encourage him to investigate his experience. Validate his description, feelings, and thoughts about the experience. Encourage him to wonder what the experience means to him. Let him tell his story, and listen to him as many times as he wants to explore it.

Withdrawal during the Dying Process

Dear Dr. Leary:

I want to connect with my dying grandmother in her last days, as she is dying from terminal cancer. But she appears to be pulling away and does not want to say the things I thought we should say to each other. She also does not seem to want me to touch her. I thought I was doing the right things, but I am hurt and confused. Please help me understand.

—Sherrie

Dear Sherrie:

You are witnessing the end stages of dying when many people withdraw as their energy wanes and their interest in this world fades, in preparation for their transition. Without intending to, they are often unable to focus or concentrate on what is going on around them, or to participate with family members in their usual way. Their skin also becomes increasingly sensitive to the touch, so that even gentle stroking feels too harsh to them. If that is the case, the simple act of gently holding their hand from beneath so they can control the pressure and duration will be of comfort to them.

The dying person's hearing is also acute, and harsh noises, loud music, or sounds that interrupt her peace are jarring and disruptive. Be sensitive to her preferences and ask her if she wants company, if she wants to be touched, or if she wants conversation or music. Make your grandmother comfortable, and maintain a sanctuary for her. Please try not to take your grandmother's physical withdrawal or inability to focus personally; she is not consciously ignoring you but is turning toward the next step in her journey. Her body and mind are going through an orderly and progressive series of changes in order to prepare the body functioning to stop. You will give her the most powerful gift and interact with her in the most loving way when you allow her to move toward death in her own way, in her own timing, and you honor her wishes. You are making a difference through your loving acts of support and validation.

❧ ❧ ❧

Is There Suffering at Death?

Dear Dr. Leary:

Did my brother suffer at the time of his death? His body looked like he was in agony.

—Carl

Dear Carl:

Your brother emerged from his body in a similar manner as the butterfly sheds its skin. As we watch the butterfly work itself out of its cocoon, we project our fears and imagine that it is a painful struggle. Your brother and the butterfly emerge through their transition into a new dimension.

We know from reports from others who have gone through the change of dying that the moments right before death are not painful or fearful or negative. The reports from thousands of people who have died and witnessed their bodies during the transition and at the moment of clinical death tell us that they leave their body and are not concerned with the shell that they leave behind.

What death looks like to the outside observer is not what it feels like on the inside to the person who is dying. They do not perceive the same struggle you imagine, though you may hear a death rattle from the throat or watch their eyes open suddenly right before death. It is your interpretation of these body responses that causes you anxiety and pain, and it is not a true reflection of what is happening to your loved one. Do not misunderstand your external experience for their internal experience. They are released, pain-free, and without fear or anxiety.

Do not believe the illusion of the transition. Do not recall your loved one from the moment of their death. Remember the living they accomplished, the love they shared, and the soul's expression rather than the body's transition.

Dying Alone

Dear Dr. Leary:

I cared for my mother for ten months as she was dying, and I stayed with her the whole time. At her insistence, I took an hour to leave and complete an errand, and that was the time that she died, the one time I was not with her. I can't stop feeling guilty about letting her down. How can I get past this feeling?

—Sharon

Dear Sharon:

How do you know that you let your mother down? Can you open to the possibility that a great wisdom within her may have chosen to die and let go of any struggle when you were not with her? Can you imagine that this might have been her last gift to you? From a mother's point of view, can you empathize with how difficult it would be to leave you, or to listen to you wail in the moment of her death?

How different would you feel about yourself, about your gift of loving care to her, and about her death . . . if you knew that the timing of her death was perfect for her? I have been with so many dying people who were companioned by family for months before their death, holding vigil and rarely leaving the dying alone. After so many incidents like theirs and yours, I was rarely surprised that the dying slipped away silently when they were alone, without the pull of loved ones and the difficulty of leaving so much love behind. Can you imagine that it was so difficult for her to leave you that she left when you were not with her?

Denial as a Coping Tool

Dear Dr. Leary:

My seventy-five-year-old sister refuses to discuss her terminal diagnosis or talk about plans for her funeral. I don't know how to help her out of denial. What should I say to her?

—Frustrated Sister

Dear Frustrated Sister:

In many situations, a dying person is aware, on a conscious or unconscious level, that they are dying. However, we must respect their emotional and psychological response to *their* process and *their* challenges. Their feelings, reactions, and responses are part of their freedom, and sometimes the greatest support we can offer is to *accept* rather than understand or agree with their response. There may be cultural, familial, spiritual, or personal reasons for their approach, but we do not have to know their reasons in order to honor and support their path.

As difficult as it may be to honor the way your sister chooses to spend her remaining time, remember that denial is a valid choice. If you have demonstrated an open attitude and a willingness to listen to whatever she wants to discuss and she chooses not to address the subject of her terminal illness or prospect of dying, do not force your needs or agenda upon her. There are many choices and ways to approach dying. There is no "one size fits all" that addresses everyone's needs, beliefs, and values.

Caregivers and family members often underestimate a person's capacity to know and cope with the truth of their prognosis. Some will demand to know all the details, while others will successfully use denial to cope and provide them with strength and hope. Denial has gotten a lot of bad press, but it is a legitimate coping style. Let's honor a loved one's wishes even when they are contrary to our own.

Despite her unwillingness to speak directly about the end of her life, you can nevertheless provide her with the love, compassion, and care she needs during this time in her life. You can offer to listen to whatever she wishes to discuss. You can advocate for her comfort, care, and pain relief. You can invite loved ones to visit with her. You can be present to her needs and wishes. In the end, you will have made a difference in how she died, even though she would not discuss the reality of dying. You both will have acted from a place of authenticity and personal values.

≈ ✂ ≈

Dealing with Your Dying Loved One's Anger

Dear Dr. Leary:

My dying father and I have had a close relationship, but as he gets weaker, I can hardly deal with his anger. He lashed out at me recently when he overheard me talking about him as a patient. I don't know what I did wrong.

—Connie

Dear Connie:

Your father may have been reacting to his increasing loss of control and identity as he gets sicker, weaker, and closer to giving up most of the control in his life. He may be feeling that he is powerless over his illness and imminent death; his body is deteriorating, and he is no longer able to contribute in roles or positions that used to give him a sense of being an important part of the world. His anger may reflect all that he is giving up and his grief about that.

The word *patient* can separate the caregiver from the person who is dying. They may hear the word as referring to someone who is put into the role of being passive, being helped, being submissive, and being an obligation. People who are dying do not want to be reminded of being helpless, limited, dependent, or "the problem."

We can give them back their identity and value by using their name instead of labels—by focusing on their strengths, life experience, wisdom, and resources. We want to take any focus off of ourselves as "fixers" so that the caregiver is never the focus of the experience. It might be helpful to see ourselves in service as a midwife or labor coach in their transition; they are doing the majority of the work, and we are there to support and assist.

If you are the target of your father's anger, one way you might think about it is that you are serving as a container for his anger. What is not *expressed* can become *depressed*. You can help him by allowing, even encouraging, him to get rid of his heavy feelings, releasing whatever is getting in the way of his feeling at peace. There are many ways to serve, and if our intention is for their highest good, we can be willing to do that which is uncomfortable for us.

Caregiving to the Unresponsive

Dear Dr. Leary:

My mother is dying and is unresponsive. My brother refuses to be with her in any way; he will not provide any of the physical care or even come into her room to sit with her or talk to her. How can I explain to him that he can still make a difference?

—Tom

Dear Tom:

You can educate your brother to the facts about an unresponsive patient. Oftentimes a person who is dying is labeled as unresponsive because they do not react or respond as we think they should or as they used to before their illness. The dying are always communicating, but we may not have the awareness to accurately read them. Even when they are not verbally or visually communicating with us, their breathing rate and sounds, the temperature and color of their skin, their level of activity, and their bodily responses all tell us something important about the person. It may also be that the dying can respond but are choosing not to, instead spending their energy focusing inward and detaching from the world around them. Whether responsive or not, your loved one deserves your attention, care, and respect.

How can you encourage your brother to communicate and share his unique expressions of care toward her? Here are some examples of ways your brother can make a difference:

1. When entering the dying person's room, acknowledge that person by name before addressing anyone else. The last sense to go is often the sense of hearing. Behave as though they hear every word.

2. Respond to any sign or response from the patient such as facial expression, movement, breathing rate, and sounds. Most of the time, we may not know what they mean, but we can ask and respond with the intention of providing comfort care.

3. As a reflection of respect, offer choices whenever possible no matter how mundane or insignificant the choices may appear. When illness or aging has deprived your loved one of health, activity, connections, and identities we can continue to offer them options and show them they still have personal power.

Remind your brother that the dying are still living, right up to the moment of their last breath. This is important to remember for your loved one as well as for the caregiver who has the opportunity to make a difference, in however small a way, to communicate love and respect. His participation is important to his dying mother, and will also be important to him in his grief.

LETTERS AND RESOURCES ON GRIEF

I write a column called *Healing Tears* for the LifeNet Health Foundation to respond to the needs of bereaved children, parents, spouses, siblings, and friends (see http://www.healingthespirit.org/newsletters/). I share these letters and stories with you in hopes that you might identify with the writers' situations and challenges, and will be able to find guidance in my responses to them.

Children Grieve Differently than Adults

Dear Dr. Leary:

I am a forty-year-old father. I lost my ten-year-old son in an accident a year ago. My primary concern right now is his brother (age nine) who is doing poorly in school, not communicating, and taking the loss really hard. What should I do?

—Stan

Dear Stan:

It sounds as though you are worried that your son may be grieving in an unhealthy way by shutting down and shutting others out. As parents and professionals, we must recognize that it is important not only how our children respond to loss but also how long before they return to some degree of normalcy. Children who are not assisted with their immense feelings of loss and through the long process of grieving may indeed find that they have grown into adulthood trapped in the limitations of a child's grief.

You are a conscientious parent to notice the decline in his academics and the ways he is disconnecting from others. You are doing the first and most important task of helping your child: you are truly seeing him and acknowledging his pain. My suggestion is to follow up with your assessment and tell him directly what you are noticing; let him know that he is seen. Include him as fully as you can in your process. My analogy is to take his hand and gently lead him as you walk your path of grief. You are both in a strange and foreign forest, and he needs rational explanations of what he is experiencing. Tell him how you are feeling your grief in your body and how you are working it out. He needs to know he is not alone. And he needs assistance to give his sorrow words. This is not asking him to do your work, or to feel your feelings, but rather to point out what you are learning and experiencing; it is like finding an unusual plant in a new forest and examining it together. Include him in rituals and remembrances. Explain the truth of what happened to his brother. Do not leave him alone to figure out his feelings. Help him find ways to express the full range of his emotions, and tell him that all his feelings are okay. Perhaps the two of you could create a photo album or memory book about his brother, using it as a platform from which to talk, laugh, and cry about him.

You might use the scrapbook or another activity such as building a fort or tending to the gravesite as a means of helping your son with the major tasks of good grief:

- To understand and begin to make sense out of what has happened
- To identify and express his strong reactions to the loss
- To commemorate the life of his brother and their relationship
- To learn how to go on living and loving without his brother

Your continual assurance and demonstration of your loving presence in his life are of the greatest value. Your patience and listening skills will communicate volumes to him. And when at a loss for words, remember to communicate by touching and holding him.

How Long Does Grief Last?

Dear Dr. Leary:

My dad has been dead eighteen months. I am still grieving and sometimes feel like it was just yesterday. Some days are especially bad. Should I be over this by now? I still can't talk about him without crying. How do I move past this and begin to live a normal life again?

—Carrie

Dear Carrie:

When we lose a loved one, the only way past the hurt is to go directly through it. Engaging in personal grief work is extremely courageous because it asks us to touch the parts of ourselves that are the most tender and most vulnerable. Grief requires us to stay in a dark place and find new meaning toward a way of life and a world that has been turned upside down by death. In order to move past the hurt, we must dive into it and (1) accept the reality of the death, (2) feel and express our reactions to the loss, (3) adjust to our life without our loved one, and (4) find a way to reinvest in life.

Our normal beliefs, worldview, and behavior may suffer for a long time. Grief asks that you find a new normal definition of life and of yourself. If we have never suffered the loss of a loved one before, death takes us by surprise and the long journey through grief feels rudderless and prolonged. Even if we have been through the heartache and questioning after the death of a loved one, each new loss requires its own journey and work.

Your grief has its own timing. It may come in waves rather than a steady gush, and it can be unpredictable or come as reminders during special times of the year.

Many mourners report that the second year is more difficult than the first. What they may be referring to is that the first year is lived in shock and disorientation, and later the body is able to adjust to the reality and begins feeling the loss and expressing it. You are not late or delayed or wrong in your grief. You are doing the hard work of accepting your father's death, reviewing the relationship, and finding a way to live without him.

Your grief is personal, and you will find your own way to express it and work through it. No one else can tell you what it should look like or sound like. Grief is not an assignment with

a due date of completion. Grief is an active, coping investment of energy and emotion, and it asks that you relearn the
world without your father. It will take time and many attempts
to redefine yourself and your roles without this loved one in
your life.

When you ask if you *should* be over your grief after only
eighteen months, you may be sentencing yourself to more
heartache through your own judgment. Our culture has unrealistic
expectations about the grieving process. We do not have mentors
or guides to model healthy grieving, and we do not know how to
observe our intense feelings without judgment. Your grief is personal, and it is your psyche's way of working through and
understanding your relationship with your father and the impact
of his death. However long you visit the stories, and whenever
thoughts of him come to mind, is part of your healing. My suggestion is to be an observer as well as a participant in your grief;
witness your tears and at the same time tell yourself, "I am okay."
As you are able to hold that awareness as well as "I am sad" and "I
am coping" at the same time, you will have more confidence and
less anxiety about experiencing your grief. You are moving into
your new life and doing it in your own perfect timing. Be patient
with yourself, please.

Grieving Is a Process

Dear Dr. Leary:

I feel overwhelmed and paralyzed by the death of my husband. I feel weak and am ashamed by the torrent of my
emotion. I doubt that I will be able to face the future, and I

don't know how to wake up in the morning without him. There are no manuals to help me get over these feelings, and I am stuck. Help!

—Cynthia

Dear Cynthia:

There is a difference between *feeling* overwhelmed and *being* overwhelmed. The reality and shock of your husband's death leaves you with thoughts, questions, and concerns that shake your foundation. The past life of security that you trusted has changed and made you look at your world in new ways. It is normal that your sense of self, sense of belonging, and sense of safety would be disturbed. One of the tasks of your grief work is to find a way to be in this world in a new way without him. That requires feeling, thought, and action.

Distinguishing the feelings of being paralyzed from the experience of being paralyzed is key to being able to regain a sense of balance and control in your life. You can begin to feel more confident and less overwhelmed in the midst of your grief by acknowledging your feelings but separating them from your experience.

You can feel afraid even while you step out and accept a challenge. You can feel hopeless even while you attend a support group. In fact, your letter to me demonstrates that in the face of feeling paralyzed, you gathered the energy and focus required to ask for help. Somehow, despite feeling paralyzed, you imagined that there might be a way through this; you asked the question, and you acted upon it. That is personal power in the middle of tragedy.

Anger, guilt, or other negative feelings can exist at the same time as more positive feelings about the person who died. In the same way, you can at the same time feel overwhelmed while able to act in a powerful way. What needs to be done? What would you do if you were not feeling overwhelmed? If you can name what needs to be done and break it down into steps, then you can begin to move forward. You do not have to do it all, but if you can do one thing differently today, you will begin to feel more powerful and less paralyzed. You can begin to write your own personal manual.

I am not suggesting that you not feel your sadness and emptiness. I am suggesting that you can hold your feelings *and* act in your best interest, even if you don't feel like you want to. Ask for help; be with others who have also lost a loved one; find a companion to shepherd you.

You may feel flooded and overwhelmed by a range of emotions, and for that you are judging yourself harshly. Perhaps you might step back and consider that your weakness is also your greatest strength, for it provides you the ability to feel connected to all the rest of us who will also grieve for loved ones. Accepting our emotions allows us to embrace our humanity.

Resistance to Moving On

Dear Dr. Leary:

I'm thinking about a move in the near future. How will I deal with being in a new place where no one knew my deceased husband? How will I keep track of him in a place where he never was? It's like losing him again.

—Cheryl

Dear Cheryl:

Yours is not an uncommon task: in the journey called grief, we must find the courage and energy to move forward into the uncharted territory of a place and time that does not include our loved one.

The feeling of losing him again is what you do as you return to the reality of his death again and again, to understand the mystery of loss from many different angles. You are returning, reviewing, and readjusting to the reality of life without him.

When we grieve, the daunting task is to relearn how to live in the world and relearn what our world is without our loved one. We have to find answers to: Who am I without him? What does my life mean without him? We have to learn how to invest ourselves in facets of life that once involved our loved one. We have to learn *who* we are now, and *how* to be ourselves in a world without our loved one to reflect and validate us.

Your relationship with your husband has been expressed and shared in ways that were seen, felt, and heard. Now you must learn how to have a different kind of relationship with him. The best metaphor I can think of is a song. You have sung a melody with your husband for years called "Marriage." Even when you are not actively singing it so others can hear it, you are able to hold it in your mind, hear it echo, and replay it anytime you choose. You carry the tune though the song does not sing itself. The song lives in you even when the singing stops . . . you can hear the echo in your mind, your heart, and your life. You carry that wherever you go in the future.

Dr. Robert Lifton talks about a "symbolic immortality" as we learn to live and acknowledge the values, meanings, and legacy left to us by the deceased. We can make our focus the mystery of the immortal aspects of their lives. The struggle is to retain and cherish what you have been given from him and your relationship. Take that and shape the future years, weaving his legacy into your new life.

Your love for your husband lives on in your mind and heart. You take that with you wherever you go. Your husband's memory and the memories of your life together can serve as the foundation and template for your future life, guiding you based on values and priorities you forged together. You will carry your husband, and the core of who you are, into your future.

Holiday Reminders

Dear Dr. Leary:

It's been eight years since our son died. This past holiday season was extremely difficult . . . our three other children and grandchildren were home. As I looked around the room on Christmas morning, my heart tugged. Stephen will never know his nieces and nephews . . . he would have been a wonderful uncle. I'm beginning to experience the what-if thoughts again, and these thoughts are more difficult than before. I feel a sense of pull going backward with my grief, and I so much want to take a step forward again.

—Anne

Dear Anne:

Perhaps we can interpret this from another perspective. It is Christmastime, and of course you think of Stephen. You are reminded of your dreams and hopes for him in many roles; his nieces and nephews remind you that he will not be able to match your dreams. Stephen's death was a loss of life, an end to your dreams for him and a life with him. Each time you encounter one of your dreams of Stephen's future you must say another good-bye and feel a new grief for that specific loss.

Through your thoughts and immense love of Stephen, you bring him back into your midst. And your perception now is that these thoughts of missing your son are more pronounced and more aching than in the beginning of your grief. But now the numbness and the shock have worn off, and your feelings of loss and vulnerability can surface and be more fully felt. You have also lived through eight years of the void of his shining presence, and you are more aware than ever that his absence in family celebrations such as this will go on forever. The "ongoingness" of grief is daunting, and yet you have experience and evidence that your grief is manageable and you have learned to live without him.

Your thoughts of "what if" are another way of circling around the reality of his death; you continue to consider what is lost and how your life is different. This is the acknowledgment and reaffirmation of so great a loss. You continue to grieve, and you are acknowledging the many reasons for that grief: Christmas is supposed to be a time of celebration, a time of family reunions, and so Stephen's absence is even more striking. And it is important to continue to acknowledge the difference his death makes in your life. Oftentimes when we let the feelings swell, verbalize them, and have them affirmed, we can then begin to step forward again.

Perhaps the pull backward is more accurately a momentum forward. If these feelings are a messenger, look to what they are asking of you. My hunch is that the feelings are asking to be known and accepted. The challenge is to have the faith to fall backward into it and the trust that your support system will catch you, hold you, and comfort you.

Think about these past eight years and remember that you have the experience and evidence from past attempts that you are able to get up after a descent into grief. I need to repeat that grief is extremely personal. It is not a linear, step-by-step process. Grief is a long-term undertaking that can reappear at any time and ask to be reworked. The question we usually ask is *Will I ever get over it?* and the answer is yes . . . and no. We can reach the time when remembering does not overwhelm us the way it did in the beginning. We heal, but we remember, and living with the memory is part of the healing.

We Each Grieve in Unique Ways

Dear Dr. Leary:

My husband and I lost our youngest child one year ago. I am really concerned about my husband. He rarely talks about our daughter's death. He mopes around his workshop and works in the garden, but he refuses to even consider the local support group I attend. What can I do to help him?

—Joan

Dear Joan:

Just as your grief and grief work are unique to you, your husband's feelings of loss, his journey through this dark night of the soul, and the meaning he attaches to your child's death are uniquely his own. You can best help him by acknowledging that he is different from you, by affirming that he has feelings and his own experience of this loss, and by allowing and encouraging him to find his own expressions of grief. That may mean his grief work does not include expressing feelings as you would easily do in words and within the network of friends. Your husband is indeed expressing his feelings, but in his actions and work in his workshop and garden. The display of your grief may be more obvious and understood in our culture, more easily recognized through words and tears. Your husband may sweat his tears in physically exhausting work or sports. Both expressions are valid, appropriate, direct, and helpful means of moving the energy of sadness, despair, confusion, anger, guilt, anxiety, and loneliness.

You can help your husband by giving him time and space to explore his new environment without your child. Support him by brainstorming opportunities for him to create or build something that honors your child. Many men find it helpful to put their grief into action, while women find it easier to put their feelings into words. Perhaps you could partner in a project that would involve him building (a playground or bench) and you writing the words for the dedication ceremony.

The greatest help with our grief comes through validation. You strengthen his connection with your child and substantiate his experiences of loss when you honor his way, his timing, his intensity, his pacing, and his unique ways of expression. *Bless his grief.* Give him permission to express his feelings, remain in character, and cope on his own terms, without judgment.

Grief is work, but the expression and completion of this grief work may be internal and invisible to others. It is important to be respectful of each person's way of grieving and not to push mourners to express grief in limited ways. If someone doesn't react as we do, it doesn't mean they feel any differently. Partners express grief at different times, with different expressions, and with different intensities. The way a person expresses their grief has little to do with the magnitude of their loss.

                                  ❧ ❧ ❧

Multiple Losses

Dear Dr. Leary:

I am having a terrible time moving forward after multiple losses (mother to cancer 2001, loss of business 2001, father to cancer in 2003, mother-in-law to cancer in 2005, father-in-law to heart attack in 2006, and most recently, my only sister). I just don't know how to move forward. I'm completely stuck. How can I move past these losses and engage in life again? I feel like an addict; I hide my grief from others.

—Mary-Anne

Dear Mary-Anne:

You are having a very difficult emotional, physical, and spiritual crisis from multiple losses over a very short period of time. All of your energies are drained with trying to make sense from the reorganization of your world and trying to find meaning from the pain. You must feel exhausted, and perhaps in your wisdom, you have retreated to gather the energy that grieving and meaning-making requires. Learning to live with all of these deaths in your life will require an acceptance of the reality, the time to review and make meaning of each loss, a network of support, and the resources of energy and mindfulness to create a new place and new identity without these loved ones in your immediate environment.

To "hide your grief from others" sounds like you feel ashamed of your feelings and your response to these life events. If you were an objective bystander observing the harsh, multiple deaths of so many loved ones within such a short period of time, would you expect a friend to get over it, get on with life, or buck up? Would you not allow, or even encourage, your friend to express her heartache, fears, and disappointment? If you will give yourself the gift of allowing what is without judgment, without expectations, and without having to understand your feelings, you will be closer to accepting the reality and power of these multiple losses.

In your isolation you have lost a sense of normalcy. If you shared your grief with others who are experiencing similar losses, you would come to see that they, like you, have felt they have lost a place in the world, lost a means of contributing, lost the family support system to belong to, lost a sense of identity, lost dreams of the future, and lost a sense of hope. You are not alone; you are not crazy; you are not wrong. To share your grief and belong to a group of mourners is to know that there is no shame in grief. I encourage you to search out a bereavement support group that might be offered through your local church, hospice, hospital, or mental health agency. You might also go online to www.griefnet.org and begin corresponding with others grieving a similar loss.

You *can* learn to live life with these losses and engage in life again one day at a time, starting in the present. Please begin today and share your grief.

Disenfranchised Grief: Suicide

Dear Dr. Leary:

My best friend's daughter recently committed suicide. I want to support my friend, but I don't know what to say or do about a suicide.

—Joe

Dear Joe:

Death by suicide and the untimely death of a child are two of the most difficult losses to adjust to. When others do not acknowledge the death, it is often because the circumstance of the death (suicide, abortion, miscarriage) is judged and the mourners are socially invisible, left to grieve in silence and alone. Sometimes the nature of the relationship with the deceased is judged in a way that allows them to dismiss, stigmatize, or deny the significance of the connection. For example, as a society we may not be as sensitive to grieving the death of adult children, the mentally challenged individual, the elderly, or an unborn child. When a homosexual partner, extramarital partner, aborted or miscarried fetus, prisoner, coworker, or friend dies, the grief might not be recognized or attended to in the same way as the death of a spouse.

Validation by others is a key to resolving our grief. We need others' acknowledgment of the importance of the relationship to the deceased as well as acknowledgment of the circumstances of the death. In one way or another, with words and actions, we need to communicate that this man's daughter was important to him. You also want to be sensitive to the sudden, unexpected nature of the death that intensifies the shock, disbelief, and lack of opportunities to prepare or say good-bye.

Those who have lived through their grief have taught me that there are ways to make a difference. Offer concrete help instead of saying, "Just call me if you need something"—bring over dinner, pick up visiting relatives, do errands, mow the yard. Offer to help with funeral arrangements or errands. Write a note, especially after a few months have passed, when others are getting on with their lives. Invite your friend out to do something you both have enjoyed in the past, and if the invitation is declined at first, offer again at a later date. Offer to be on call in the middle of the night if your friend cannot sleep and would find it helpful to talk then. Call the person and include them in activities.

One of the most helpful things we can do for others is to put aside our notions of what good grief looks like and not make assumptions. Ask, inquire, and allow for the ebbs and surges of your friend's grief. It takes so much energy to grieve, and the last thing that a grieving person needs is to feel that they must fulfill others' expectations. Be willing to just be there in whatever way your friend might find it comforting.

The death of a child is different from other deaths and must be respected as such. Do not compare it with the loss of your parent, spouse, or pet. The grief of a bereaved parent is not contagious; do not shy away or fail to offer the comfort of touch. If your friend cries, do not assume that you have hurt him; allow him to feel his feelings that have nothing to do with you. Realize that his child has died and that is the cause of his tears. Crying and emotional catharsis are healing and helpful.

You can help your friend by sharing memories, remembering to speak his daughter's name and to talk about her with specific stories and details. Encourage him to talk about her and tell stories as often as he wants to, even repeating the same stories as necessary. If your friend is more comfortable releasing his grief physically rather than verbally, help him to express his grief through action and suggest ways that the two of you might sweat his grief, such as building a memorial to her, organizing a fund-raising road race, writing a song, or planting a memorial garden.

I Can Find Meaning in Loss

Dear Dr. Leary:

My son died a little over six months ago in a car accident. He was twenty-four, so full of life—a recent college grad, engaged to be married, and employed at a job he enjoyed. I am finding it very difficult to participate in church activities. I am still angry and disappointed with God, although at times I feel guilt about this—I just can't stand the biblical platitudes and phrases as a source of comfort. Will this change?

—June

Dear June:

It sounds like you are trying to make sense of your terribly painful loss in the midst of normal expectations. Most of us have assumptions that the young die after the elderly, that children die after parents, that good things come to those full of life and promise. And that God keeps our loved ones from danger.

The tragedy does not make sense to you, and you are experiencing cognitive dissonance. You may feel as though your son has been cheated and robbed of his future, and you have lost your hopes and dreams of a future and a legacy. You are trying to understand how God and/or life could have *not* met your expectations and dreams. What has happened to you goes against all of your values, beliefs, and goals for your life and that of your loved ones.

Your son's death was sudden, unexpected, and untimely. Losing a child is one of the most painful and disorienting experiences a person will ever face. Anger is a normal and common expression of grief. Anger can be directed at others, at God, or at a disease. You are expressing anger and disillusionment with a belief system that once supported you and now feels empty. Death shakes our core, and part of the grief work is to make sense of and find meaning in the loss. You are still working through that and trying to find peace. Right now the church that once comforted you and gave you meaning feels empty, and you do not find solace in ways that previously gave you peace.

It is difficult to find the energy to reach out and ask for help from others. If you know that the biblical platitudes are not comforting, perhaps you can ask directly for what you know to be of help. A sincere embrace from a friend is often more soothing than a lecture about love. You have the right to maintain boundaries and talk about your son with only those you choose. Working through your grief may require time off from work and restoring yourself with attention in other activities if you are able.

It is normal to reexamine our beliefs, values, and faith after such a devastating death. It is a strengthening and necessary exercise to question our foundation in order to come to some integration and understanding of the nature of life, or of a higher power. You need time and encouragement to untangle your grief from your beliefs, without any feelings of pressure or guilt. You will not always be angry, disappointed, and struggling. But everyone's timing and grief work is different due to many factors such as social support, personality, the relationship with the deceased, and previous experiences with loss. As you work through this difficult time of adjustment to accept your son's death, the intensity of your grief will soften, the frequency of grief surges will lessen, and your ability to cope will strengthen. I encourage you to honor your own pace, find supportive people or groups that allow you to grieve in your unique way, and reinvest by developing a different relationship and an enriched remembrance with your precious son.

Disenfranchised and Unacknowledged Grief

Dear Dr. Leary:

My baby girl died at birth. Family members try to console me by saying that I will get over my grief because I didn't have too much time to become attached and had not invested too much. I feel as though they are telling me that my child was not real enough to me. This makes me feel outraged as well as devastated. Can you help me?

—Cindy

Dear Cindy:

Your grief is every bit as deep and profound as if you had nurtured your child into adulthood. Your outrage comes from having your grief unacknowledged, diminished, and not validated.

Others, who have not lost a child, do not understand the magnitude or meaning of your loss.

What you are experiencing from others who dismiss or minimize your loss is called "disenfranchised grief." It is grief that is not recognized and not legitimized in our society. It is not deemed as real as other losses and so is not given the same respect, significance, or rituals as other deaths.

The nature of your loss is sudden, and that factor compounds the difficulty of your grief. The suddenness, lack of anticipation, and inability to prepare for the death leave you with feelings of being out of control and without support systems. Unlike the opportunities in an anticipated death such as terminal illness, you were not given the opportunity to say good-bye, to contribute to the care of your loved one, to understand the cause of death, to struggle with questions and begin to find meaning, or to connect with social agencies for support.

One of the most important questions a grief therapist can ask a mourner is: To what extent, if any, had you expected the death of your loved one? The answer guides caregivers with what strategies might be helpful.

The meaning of your loss is great. Your child has died. Your legacy, your hopes, and your dreams for the future have been buried. At this time, whether you have more children or not, your name and your identity as a parent have died with that child. You are grieving the loss of your child and all the hopes for the future attached to your child.

Next to our physical survival, the greatest need we have is our need to be understood, to be affirmed, to be validated, and to have our experience appreciated. Our most difficult times in grief are when our pain is not understood or permitted; when it is shunned or avoided, or our loss is deemed less than that of others.

You need to hear from others that your grief is real and valid, and that it is okay to not be okay. The physical presence of a friend and an ongoing relationship of support are what will help right now. Perhaps you can take this article to someone who asks you what he or she can do for you. If you can find one person who will genuinely listen to your pain as often as you need to talk about it, rather than give you advice, you will be on your way toward healing. It is a lifelong journey, and only you can do it, but you do not have to be alone.

Further Reading Resources

Byock, I. *Dying Well: The Prospect for Growth at the End of Life* (New York: Putnam, 1997).

Fitzgerald, H. *The Grieving Child: A Parent's Guide*, 2nd ed. (New York: Simon & Schuster, 2003).

Fitzgerald, H. *The Mourning Handbook: A Complete Guide for the Bereaved* (New York: Simon & Schuster, 1995).

Frankl, V. E. *Man's Search for Meaning* (New York: Simon & Schuster, 1997).

Fulghum, R. *True Love: Stories Told to and by Robert Fulghum* (New York: HarperCollins, 1997).

Goldman, L. *Life and Loss: A Guide to Help Grieving Children*, 2nd ed. (New York: Taylor and Francis, 2000).

Kübler-Ross, E. *On Death and Dying* (New York: Macmillan, 1969).

Kushner, H. *When Bad Things Happen to Good People* (New York: Schocken Books, 1981).

Levine, S. *Meetings at the Edge: Dialogues with the Grieving and the Dying, the Healing and the Healed* (New York: Anchor, 1984).

Rando, T. *How to Go On Living When Someone You Love Dies* (New York: Random House, 1991).

Silverman, P. R. *Widow to Widow: How the Bereaved Help One Another* (New York: Psychology Press, 2004).

Novels and Personal Stories about Grief for Adults

Albom, M. *Tuesdays with Morrie: An Old Man, a Young Man, and Life's Greatest Lesson* (New York: Doubleday, 1997).

Barthes, R., and R. Howard. *Mourning Diary* (New York: Hill & Wang, 2010).

Berg, E. *Talk Before Sleep* (New York: Random House, 1994).

Didion, J. *The Year of Magical Thinking* (New York: Knopf, 2005).

Lewis, C. S. *A Grief Observed* (New York: HarperCollins, 1961).

Noel, C. *In the Unlikely Event of a Water Landing: A Geography of Grief* (New York: Times Books, 1996).

Oates, J. C. *A Widow's Story* (New York: Ecco, 2011).

O'Rourke, M. *The Long Goodbye* (New York: Riverhead, 2011).

Rieff, D. *Swimming in a Sea of Death: A Son's Memoir* (New York: Simon & Schuster, 2008).

Roiphe, A. R. *Epilogue: A Memoir* (New York: Harper Perennial, 2009).

Winston, L. *Good Grief* (New York: Warner Books, 2004).

Books to Explain Death and Grief to Children

Alley, R. W. and M. Mundy. *Sad Isn't Bad: A Good-Grief Guidebook for Kids Dealing with Loss* (Indiana: Abbey Press, 1998). Healthy grief model.

Buscaglia, L. F. *The Fall of Freddie the Leaf: A Story of Life for All Ages* (New York: Slack Inc., 1982). All things die.

Coerr, E., and R. Himler. *Sadako and the Thousand Paper Cranes* (New York: Penguin, 2004). How to help and grieve.

dePaola, T. *Nana Upstairs & Nana Downstairs* (New York: Putnam, 1973). Death of grandparents.

Fry, V. L. *Part of Me Died, Too: Stories of Creative Survival among Bereaved Children and Teenagers* (New York: Dutton Children's Books, 1995). Loss of pet, sister, mother with AIDS, abusive father; creative activities to explore feelings; ages 10–18.

Grollman, E. *Talking about Death: A Dialogue between Parent and Child* (Boston: Beacon, 1991). Parents' guide to discussing death.

Krementz, J. *How It Feels When a Parent Dies* (New York: Knopf, 1981). Death of a parent.

Miles, M. *Annie and the Old One* (Boston: Little, Brown & Co., 1971). Death of grandparent.

Nystrom, C. *Emma Says Goodbye* (Oxford, England: Lion Pub. Corp., 1990). Hospice, dying at home.

Paterson, K. *Bridge to Terabithia* (New York: HarperCollins, 1977). Death of a friend; ages 10+.

Schwiebert, P., and C. DeKlyen. *Tear Soup* (Portland, OR: Grief Watch, 1999). How to grieve in your own unique way.

Varley, S. *Badger's Parting Gifts* (New York: HarperCollins, 1992). Death of friend.

Viorst, J. *The Tenth Good Thing About Barney* (New York: Aladdin, 1987). Death of pet.

Wilhelm, H. *I'll Always Love You* (New York: Crown, 1988). Death of pet.

Wise Brown, M. *The Dead Bird* (St. Louis, MO: Turtleback Books, 1999). Picture book for the very young.

Links to Bereavement Resources and Support for Children

- The Dougy Center: www.dougy.org
  Through the National Center for Grieving Children and Families, the Dougy Center provides support and training locally to Portland,

Oregon; nationally and internationally to individuals and organizations seeking to assist children in grief.

- Mourning Star Center: www.mourningstar.org
A nonprofit support center for grieving children and those who love them, providing loving support in a safe place where grieving children can share their experience as they move through their healing process.
- Amanda the Panda: www.amandathepanda.org
Amanda the Panda provides support to grieving children and their families through a variety of services, including weekend camps, support groups, home visits, fun days, school presentations, holiday cheer boxes, pen pal programs, and more.
- Support Kids: www.allkidsgrieve.org
Access to individuals, organizations, materials, and ideas that facilitate the possibility of growing through loss and grief for kids and adults who care for them.
- Kara: www.kara-grief.org
Kara offers emotional support and helpful information to adults, teenagers, and children who are grieving a death or coping with a life-threatening illness.
- KIDSAID: www.kidsaid.com
KIDSAID is a site to kids, for kids, by kids for grief support and peer support, and for kids to express themselves through artwork, stories, and poetry.

Links to Bereavement Resources and Support for Adults

- AARP: www.aarp.org/relationships/grief-loss/
Resources and information for the bereaved.
- Survivors of Suicide (SOS): www.survivorsofsuicide.com
Support for the bereaved of death by suicide.

- CaringBridge: www.caringbridge.org
  Websites for family and friends that connect people experiencing a
  significant health challenge.
- GriefNet.org: www.griefnet.org
  Internet community of people dealing with loss and grief.
- Healing the Spirit: www.healingthespirit.org
  For all who mourn and are coping with the death of a loved one.
- WidowNet: www.widownet.org
  Self-help resources for and by those who have lost a life partner.
- The Compassionate Friends: www.thecompassionatefriends.org
  Support organization for bereaved parents, grandparents, and
  siblings.
- National Organization for Victim Assistance: www.trynova.org
  Promoting rights and services for victims of crime and crisis
  everywhere.
- National SUID/SIDS Resource Center: www.sidscenter.org
  Providing resources to states, communities, professionals, and fami-
  lies to reduce sudden unexpected infant death (SUID)/sudden
  infant death syndrome (SIDS) and promote healthy outcomes.
- Parents of Murdered Children: www.pomc.com
  A group dedicated to helping the families and friends of those who
  have lost their lives to violence.
- Parents without Partners: www.parentswithoutpartners.org
  Offers support, information, and resources for single parents.
- Pet Loss Grief Support: www.petloss.com
  A gentle and compassionate website for pet lovers who are grieving
  over the death of a pet or an ill pet.
- The Association for Pet Loss and Bereavement: www.aplb.org
  A network of professionally trained volunteers in pet bereavement
  counseling.
- SHARE Pregnancy and Infant Loss Support, Inc.: www.national
  share.org

Share serves those who have experienced the death of a baby due to early pregnancy loss or stillbirth, or in the first few months of life.
- Society of Military Widows: www.militarywidows.org
Supports widows of career military members, helping them to return to the mainstream of normal living.

APPENDIX C

RESOURCES AND NOTES FOR CAREGIVERS (PROFESSIONAL, FAMILY, VOLUNTEER)

Currently, 29 percent of the American population, more than sixty-five million people, are caregivers for a chronically ill, disabled, or aged loved one. The need for this service is expected to rise as the population ages and financial resources are stretched. Family caregivers are the silent foundation and bedrock of a country's healthcare system, including long-term care. The role of caregiver is often suddenly thrust upon a family member who has little training or experience in the rigors and complex needs of the patient. The following guidelines may serve as a primer for caregiving:

- Respectful listening and purposeful silence are usually more helpful than speaking.
- We fail to truly listen to the dying person if instead, when they need us to listen, we offer advice, try to fix the way they feel, do something for them that they need or want to do for themselves, or try to make sense of something that appears irrational to us but merely needs to be accepted. Instead, just listen.

- There are no perfect decisions; the priority should be the dying person's values, preferences, and choices. Every decision has advantages and gifts, disadvantages and costs.
- When in doubt about what to do, show love, acceptance, and compassion. There is always more to give.
- Remember that you and your goals are not more important than the person you serve.
- When you think or say, "I do not understand why he would do/want/think that," it usually means, "I do not like their choice."
- A person in distress needs your support. Let them talk without interrupting, interpreting, or analyzing. Let them tell the same story a hundred times if it helps them.
- Show empathy rather than sympathy to the dying and the grieving.
- We cannot know what is best for another person, but we can inquire and then support their choices. Trust another person's journey, even if it differs from your own.
- Remember and respond in a way that demonstrates that the dying are living, and the living will die. The dying person is not separate from the living but is someone experiencing a part of life that we all will experience. Pay attention and be present to each moment.

Helpful Links for Caregivers

- Americans for Better Care of the Dying: www.abcd-caring.org
  An organization that shares expertise, builds collaborative networks and public commitment to achieve substantive healthcare reform through improved policy, professional practice, and care reimbursement.
- Association for Death Education and Counseling: www.adec.org
  An international, professional organization that promotes diversity in death education, care of the dying, grief counseling, and research in thanatology.

- Family Caregiving 101: www.familycaregiving101.org
  A site offering answers, ideas, and advice for anyone caring for a loved one who is ill or disabled.
- Helpguide: www.helpguide.org
  A site that provides free online resources to understand, prevent, and resolve many of life's challenges.
- National Family Caregivers Association: www.nfcacares.org
  A site that educates, supports, empowers, and speaks up for the more than sixty-five million Americans who provide care for loved ones with a chronic illness or disability or the frailties of old age.
- Medline Plus: Health Information for Caregivers: www.nlm.nih.gov/medlineplus/caregivers.html
  A site offering information about diseases, conditions, and wellness issues from the world's largest medical library, the National Library of Medicine.
- National Caregivers Library: www.caregiverslibrary.org
  An extensive library of articles, checklists, forms, and links to topic-specific resources.
- Five Wishes: www.agingwithdignity.org/five-wishes.php
  A site to help people make end-of-life decisions and institute them as a legal living will with online support to immediately print a personalized document.
- Today's Seniors Network, "First State-by-State 'Report Card' on Care for the Dying Finds Mediocre Care Nationwide": www.todaysseniorsnetwork.com/failing_to_care_for_dying.htm
  One-stop source for news, reviews, and social developments for seniors and end-of-life care.
- Cancer Care: www.cancercare.org
  Counseling and support groups, educational publications and workshops, and financial assistance are provided by professional oncology social workers and are offered completely free of charge to

help individuals and families better cope with and manage the emotional and practical challenges arising from cancer.

- ElderHope: www.elderhope.com
  A site providing information, advance directives, and geriatric and end-of-life support for the elderly, the dying, and their caregivers and families.
- Hospice Foundation of America: www.hospicefoundation.org
  End-of-life resources for professionals, patients, and families.
- Hospice Education Institute: www.hospiceworld.org
  A not-for-profit organizational site, serving members of the public and healthcare professionals with information and education about caring for the dying and the bereaved.
- National Cancer Institute: www.cancer.gov
  Comprehensive cancer information from the U.S. government's principal agency for cancer research.
- National Hospice and Palliative Care Organization: www.nhpco.org
  Provides a search for hospice and palliative care, as well as statistics, resources, and information.
- WebMD: www.webmd.com
  Timely medical information, sources, support groups, and discussions about all health and end-of-life issues.
- Growth House: www.growthhouse.org/death.html
  A source for information about end-of-life care including resources for death and dying, hospice and palliative care, grief, and related topics.
- Selfhelp Magazine, "Death": www.selfhelpmagazine.com/articles/loss/index.shtml
  Online articles, blogs, forums, features, and self-help products to address end-of-life issues and needs.

APPENDIX D

NOTES AND CURRENT RESEARCH ON NEAR-DEATH EXPERIENCES

There have been many contributions to the study of death and dying since Dr. Elisabeth Kübler-Ross began exposing the needs and experiences of the dying. One is a major shift that has taken place because of the research into near-death experiences; that shift moves us from resistance that comes from an external, fearful view of death by observers to an internal, peaceful view by the dying of the continuity of their consciousness.

Dr. Kenneth Ring and Dr. Bruce Greyson lead the charge as researchers, educators, and pioneers in the field of near-death studies. Dr. Ring's seminal work, *Heading Toward Omega: In Search of the Meaning of the Near-Death Experience*, continues to influence and expand our understanding of the experience of dying and its impact on our evolution. Central to Ring's findings is that those who have died tell us that how they experienced their death is not at all how it appeared to others: "What death looks like is not what it feels like." And research excerpted from Greyson's chapter on near-death experiences in the book *Varieties of Anomalous Experience: Examining the Scientific Evidence* suggests the following:

- NDEs occur to people in a variety of situations, including actual clinical death or situations involving medical procedure, severe illness, injury, accident, or suicide attempt in which death is occurring, is imminent, or is possible, or in which the person believes they are about to die or are dying.
- The content of most NDEs ranges from pleasant to blissful, including common elements such as an out-of-body experience, movement through a tunnel or void, encountering deceased loved ones and supernatural beings, and a life review.
- The content of some NDEs ranges from mildly to extremely distressing, involving such content as feelings of guilt, remorse, fear, confusion, or resistance; profound isolation; or, most rarely, hellish settings.
- Immediate reactions to NDEs can range from "no big deal" to intense preoccupation.
- Long-term effects of NDEs typically involve mild to extreme changes in personal beliefs, attitudes, values, goals, and sense of spirituality.[1]

Professional caregivers provide support and service when they have accurate information, a respectful attitude, and specific skills. The most supportive caregiver encourages a safe psychological environment. In this environment, the person who has had the near-death experience can explore and express the experience and his or her evolving response to it. The caregiver creates this environment through an attitude of:

- Willingness to listen to as little or as much as the person wants to disclose
- Respect for another's personal beliefs and values that may differ from one's own
- Acceptance of the person's experience as their subjective reality

- Interest in the person as a valid human experience
- Inquiry into any meaning that the person attributes to the experience
- Support for the person's ongoing process of an evolving understanding

The following are helpful communication skills that promote acceptance and integration of the experience:

- Be willing to explain that a medical procedure may have elicited an NDE, and offer your interest and reassurance that you are open to whatever they have experienced and want to talk about.
- Reassure the person that memories may come up at any time and seem unusual or extraordinary, and you are open to listening at any time throughout their illness.
- If your loved one begins to tell you an out-of-the-ordinary memory or experience, use the skills of reflection and open questioning to help her express whatever, and as much as, she wants to explore. Restate the content and emotions of what is said, and ask questions that elicit deeper responses, rather than questions that can only be answered with yes-or-no answers.
- Help the person wonder about the meaning of their experience. If the person reports an unusual memory or experience, whether or not it seems to be an NDE, you can ask: "What does the experience mean to you?" or "How do you make sense of it?"
- If the person wants more information, you can refer him to the IANDS website: www.iands.org, which offers resources such as contact information for IANDS support groups, articles on NDE-related topics, a bibliography of near-death experiences, and audio recordings of presentations from past IANDS conferences available for purchase.

Further Reading Resources

Atwater, P. M. H. *Near-Death Experiences, The Rest of the Story: What They Teach Us About Living and Dying and Our True Purpose* (Newburyport, MA: Hampton Roads Publishing, 2011).

Atwater, P. M. H. *The Big Book of Near-Death Experiences: The Ultimate Guide to What Happens When We Die* (Newburyport, MA: Hampton Roads Publishing, 2007).

Atwater, P. M. H. *Beyond the Light: What Isn't Being Said About Near Death Experience* (Kill Devil Hills, NC: Transpersonal Publishing, 2009).

Brinkley, D., and P. Perry. *Saved by the Light: The True Story of a Man Who Died Twice and the Profound Revelations He Received* (New York: HarperCollins, 2008).

Callanan, M., and P. Kelley. *Final Gifts: Understanding the Special Awareness, Needs, and Communication of the Dying* (New York: Bantam, 1993).

Carter, C. *Science and the Near-Death Experience: How Consciousness Survives Death* (Rochester, VT: Inner Traditions, 2010).

Greyson, B., and B. Harris. "Clinical Approaches to the Near-Death Experience." *Journal of Near-Death Studies* 6 (1987): 41–52.

Kircher, P. M. *Love Is the Link: A Hospice Doctor Shares Her Experience of Near-Death and Dying* (Burdett, NY: Larson, 1995).

Kübler-Ross, E. *On Life after Death,* rev. ed. (Berkeley, CA: Celestial Arts, 2008).

Long, J., and P. Perry. *Evidence of the Afterlife: The Science of Near-Death Experiences* (San Francisco: HarperOne, 2011).

Moody, R. *Glimpses of Eternity: An Investigation Into Shared Death Experiences* (London: Rider, 2011).

Moody, R., and E. Kübler-Ross. *Life After Life: The Investigation of a Phenomenon—Survival of Bodily Death* (San Francisco: HarperOne, 2001).

Morse, M., and P. Perry. *Closer to the Light: Learning from Children's Near-Death Experiences* (New York: Villard, 1990).

Ring, K., *Mindsight: Near-Death and Out-of-Body Experiences in the Blind* (Palo Alto, CA: Institute of Transpersonal Psychology, 1999).

Ring, K., and E. Valarino. *Lessons from the Light: What We Can Learn from the Near-Death Experience* (Needham, MA: Moment Point Press, 1998).

Sharp, K. C. *After the Light: The Spiritual Path to Purpose* (New York: Avon, 1996).

Van Lommel, P. *Consciousness Beyond Life: The Science of the Near-Death Experience* (San Francisco: HarperOne, 2011).

Wills-Brandon, C. *One Last Hug Before I Go: The Mystery and Meaning of Deathbed Visions* (Deerfield Beach, FL: HCI, 2000).

Links on Near-Death Experiences

- International Association for Near-Death Studies: www.iands.org IANDS encourages independent research into NDEs and education about near-death and similar experiences.
- Near-Death Experiences and the Afterlife: www.near-death.com A website with large amounts of information on NDEs and links to other websites.
- Near-Death Experience Research Foundation: www.nderf.org The largest near-death experience website, with over 2,500 personal accounts.

∽ ⋈ ∽

Letters on Near-Death Experiences

Effects of a Near-Death Experience

Dear Dr. Leary:

My wife and I lost our son at birth during a complicated delivery. She lost consciousness, and the baby died. When my wife came to, she knew before I could tell her that our baby had died, but she did not have and has not had the normal grief I would expect, and that I feel. She told me she saw the baby being delivered to a loving presence and knew that our baby is being cared for. How can I talk to her about our loss when she does not seem to be grieving?

—Grieving Dad

Dear Grieving Dad:

Rather than having expectations about how she will feel after this experience, you can ask her open-ended questions as a way of joining her and understanding her perspective. The following questions might begin to help you both gain insight into how her experience has affected her:

1. What did you experience, and what insight did it give you that has helped you cope with losing our son?

2. What feelings do you have about the experience?

3. What did you learn from the experience that can help me with my grief?

4. How has the experience changed how you view the world around you?

People who have had near-death experiences often are confronted with doubt, skepticism, or medical explanations rather than support through listening and validation. The experience provides comfort, context, and meaning that should not be discounted, ignored, or explained away. The greatest validation for her experience is in the way she is able to live her life and to find meaning, purpose, and happiness despite the death of your son.

How to Talk about a Near-Death Experience

Dear Dr. Leary:

My six-year-old son was hospitalized and underwent a serious operation. As he was recovering, he matter-of-factly told us that during the operation, he talked with his grandmother, whom he has never met because she died before he was born. I don't know how to respond to him, and I don't know if I can believe him or if this was an aftereffect of anesthesia. What should I say to him?

—Worried Mother

Dear Worried Mother:

It is as though your son has returned from an excursion to a country you have not yet visited. The best way that you can respond to him is to listen with respect and an open mind. Allow him to talk about his experience when he wants and to process his feelings about it as often as he needs to. You do not need to have answers, interpretations, or any opinions about what he tells you. Over time and through reflection, your son will come to find his own meaning for his experience.

While your son may have been under anesthesia during his procedure, his experience is not the result of medication or from a psychotic break with reality. Your son's reaction to his experience may be powerful, confusing, and at times over-whelming as he works to make sense of it. He may tuck it away, as a young child, and come to realize its significance later in life. Some people have difficulty adjusting back in the world and feel disoriented, euphoric, or withdrawn. All are normal reactions, and you can be of great help to your young son by helping him express his experience and his feelings through words, drawing, play, or movement.

The first discussion of their near-death experience is an important process and helps them to begin to integrate their experience into their normal life; research has shown that this process can take years. Ask your son open-ended questions rather than questions that elicit a yes-or-no answer. Ask him for descriptions and feelings of the experience. Reassure him that you are interested in whatever memories come up for him, whenever they arise. Let him recount the experience as often as he wants to, and help him to find words that will explain the meaning or import of the event.

If it appears that he has difficulty adjusting after too long a period, your son may need professional guidance or a recom-mendation of a therapist who is trained to address these issues; the International Association for Near-Death Studies maintains a list of qualified therapists and may be able to make a recom-mendation in your area.

NOTES

1. Information about near-death experiences can be found on the International Association for Near-Death Studies website at www.iands.org, in its peer-reviewed scholarly research journal *Journal of Near-Death Studies*, at local IANDS group meetings, and at its annual international conferences. A comprehensive bibliography is included in its list of resources.

Bruce Greyson, MD, "Near-Death Experiences," in *Varieties of Anomalous Experience: Examining the Scientific Evidence,* Etzel Cardena, Steven J. Lynn, and Stanley Krippner, eds. (Washington, DC: American Psychological Association, 2000), 315.

In 1982 pollster George Gallup Jr. and author William Proctor released *Adventures in Immortality,* a book about near-death experiences based on two Gallup polls specifically addressing near-death experiences. The polls remain the most widely used source for statistics about NDEs.

Gallup and Proctor found that 15 percent of all Americans who had been in near-death situations reported NDEs. Of those, 9 percent included a "classic out-of-body experience," while 11 percent included entering another realm or dimension, and 8 percent featured the presence of spiritual beings. Other researchers, whose studies are usually on a smaller scale, report statistics on NDEs that can vary widely from the 1982 poll.

APPENDIX E

NOTES AND CURRENT RESEARCH ON AFTER-DEATH COMMUNICATION

Research and anecdotal stories about after-death communication from thousands of bereaved people provide comfort and emotional healing after the death of a loved one. After-death communication (ADC) is common and unremarkable in many cultures across the world, where it is socially acceptable and spoken of routinely. Because of the implications for dying without fear, recovering from trauma, and working through the tasks of grief, information on ADCs should be shared. Research by Bill and Judy Guggenheim suggests that at least fifty million Americans, or nearly 20 percent of the population, have had a spontaneous after-death communication.[1]

The ADC is defined as:

- Sensing a presence: the most commonly reported contact
- Hearing a voice: hearing an external or internal voice of the deceased
- Feeling a touch: reminiscent of the loved one's hand or embrace
- Smelling a fragrance: a favorite perfume, food, or their personal scent

- Vision: seeing the image of the deceased in either a two- or a three-dimensional space
- Twilight or asleep experiences: the presence in an alpha state or a deep-sleep state but more than a normal dream

Further Reading Resources

Guggenheim, B., and J. Guggenheim. *Hello from Heaven!* (New York: Bantam, 2005).

LaGrand, L. *After Death Communication: Final Farewells* (St. Paul, MN: Llewellyn Publications, 1998).

LaGrand, L. *Love Lives On: Learning from the Extraordinary Encounters of the Bereaved* (New York: Berkley Books, 2006).

Moody, R., and P. Perry. *Glimpses of Eternity: Sharing a Loved One's Passage from This Life to the Next* (Harlan, IA: Guideposts, 2010).

Links on After-Death Communication

- After Death Communication Research Foundation: www.adcrf.org
- The International Conference On After Death Communication: www.afterdeathconference.org

Letters on After-Death Communication

Signs of After-Death Communication

Dear Dr. Leary:

My twenty-year-old daughter died two years ago. Several times since then, I have felt her presence with me; once when I was sleeping, I felt as if I was actually walking with her. Are these thoughts anything to be concerned about?

—Steve

Dear Steve:

These experiences are more common than we acknowledge in our culture. Your intuitive sense of your daughter's presence is one of the most frequent encounters reported by the bereaved. After-death communications (ADCs) include sensing the presence of the deceased, feeling a touch, smelling a fragrance, hearing the voice of or seeing the deceased, and meeting the deceased in a vision or dream that feels real. In a National Opinion Research Center poll, 42 percent of adults reported that they "felt as though they were really in touch with someone who had died."[2] Many studies indicate that equal numbers of both sexes experience after-death communication, but more women report the experience than men. In the research I conducted for the SIDS Alliance Annual Meeting in 1997, I found that 86 percent of parents whose child died reported having an after-death communication with them in one form or another.[3]

The significance of these findings is that the bereaved found that the experience provided them a sense of comfort, a new awareness, emotional healing, and a profound sense of peace. The experience also allows the bereaved to work through another task of grief, to emotionally relocate and develop a new relationship with the deceased. The majority of bereaved who experienced an ADC was convinced that the experience was real and that they had received a meaningful gift of communication.

There appears to be a consistent purpose and theme to the communication. Most report that they were left with a message that their loved one was expressing, such as "I am okay," "I love you," or "I am with you." The bereaved who receive a spontaneous connection with their deceased loved one report that they are able to "finally rest" and have a renewed faith that they continue to have a relationship with their loved one. Though physically changed, the love continues.

After-death communication is an accepted phenomenon in other parts of the world and in other cultures and religious faiths. Most societies believe that the deceased continues his relationships with the living, and in most cultures these relationships are believed to be beneficial. Given the number of Americans who reported similar experiences, it is time we brought after-death communication into the open and allowed ourselves the comfort and validation it provides.

How has this experience affected your life? Has it affected the intensity of your grief? Has this dream brought you comfort? Have you felt a sense of peace when sensing her presence? Have these experiences disrupted your life or enhanced it? As a professional grief therapist, I would be concerned about these experiences if you were experiencing a complicated grief in which you became stuck and your grief work was not progressing. This would exhibit itself if you were not able to accept the reality of the death of your daughter, if you had a lasting loss of patterns of social interaction, if your actions were detrimental to your own social and economic health, or you displayed prolonged guilt, hostility, or somatic distress.

Studies indicate that your experience is more normal than we have been led to believe or talk about. I hope your experience with your daughter comforts you and helps you as you adjust and move into a new relationship with her.

Sensory Indications of After-Death Communication

Dear Dr. Leary:

I have smelled my wife's cologne and felt her presence, even though she has been dead ten years. How do I make sense of this?

—John

Dear John:

Before death, a dying person often becomes aware of the presence of a deceased loved one and feels comforted by their visit. The dying person may converse with the deceased and report receiving messages from them. These experiences are different from hallucinations because the dying person who is experiencing this is aware of their ordinary surroundings and the people present at the same time they are aware of the extraordinary appearance of the deceased.

In a similar way, you are experiencing after-death communication from a distinctive scent associated with your wife. Others report seeing their loved one or hearing their voice, or feeling that a loved one has visited during a dream. The experience of the deceased person's presence can range from a vague but definite feeling to a distinctive smell associated with the deceased, from hearing the deceased person's voice to seeing all or part of the deceased person, either vaguely or extremely clearly. They may also experience the presence of the deceased loved one symbolically through such common signs as butterflies, rainbows, birds and other animals, flowers, and through inanimate objects such as pictures. It is common for the bereaved to experience the presence of loved ones for the first year or so after the death, and this communication may occur throughout a lifetime, especially at times when it would be most helpful. In fact, people have reported being warned of impending danger by deceased loved ones, even after those loved ones have been dead for several years.

NOTES

1. Bill and Judy Guggenheim, *Hello from Heaven!* (New York: Bantam, 2005).

2. Attributed to Andrew Greeley, sociologist, journalist, and Catholic priest. He is a professor of sociology at the University of Arizona and is a research associate with the National Opinion Research Center at the University of Chicago. In 1989 he reported that according to a poll conducted by the National Opinion Research Center (NORC), 42 percent of Americans said that at least once they'd felt that they "were really in touch with someone who had died." Greeley further investigated a NORC poll to determine the response from widowed subjects. Of the 149 widowed respondents, the proportion of widows reporting contact with the dead "at least once or twice" was 64 percent.

3. While conducting research on pediatric psychosocial adjustment and long-term survival of HIV at the National Institutes of Health in 1996, we found that 86 percent of parents whose child died reported having an after-death communication in one form or another. The consistent report from parents was that asking the question whether they had any contact after death from their deceased child, listening to their experience, and validating their feelings was a healing and positive experience. Those exchanges taught me to incorporate that line of inquiry into subsequent work with persons grieving the loss of a loved one.

   Haven B. Battles and Lori S. Wiener, "From Adolescence through Young Adulthood: Psychosocial Adjustment Associated with Long-Term Survival of HIV," *Journal of Adolescent Health* 30, no. 3 (March 2002), 161–68.

A CAREGIVER'S BREATHING MEDITATION

Meditation can be useful for quieting a chattering mind and increasing inner peace. As a caregiver with many responsibilities and limited resources, meditation can serve to clear the mind, improve concentration, decrease stress, alleviate anxiety, and help you focus on the here-and-now. For those new to meditation, it may be easier to begin if someone verbally guides you through sequences to slow your breathing and quiet your mind. This can be accomplished by someone reading this meditation sequence to you, or recording this meditation on tape. Many guided meditations are also available on the internet with both verbal instructions and visual sequences to lead you to a deeper relaxation. This is a simple meditation you can memorize after a few practices and then do silently on your own.

> *Begin by noticing your loved one's breathing, the rise and fall of his chest, and the sound as he exhales, however gently. Put all of your attention on his breathing, and begin to breathe with him, following his pace and his rhythm. With each in-breath, invite love to fill you. With each out-breath,*

release that love and share the energy with him like a soft blanket enveloping him. Continue to breathe, in and out, with your loved one so that all of your awareness and all of your intention is on his breath.

Now with each breath in, imagine your heart expanding as your lungs expand and make room for whatever forgiveness needs to happen in order to feel at peace. It does not have to make sense, and you do not even have to name what the forgiveness is about, but allow space inside yourself for the energy of forgiveness to take up residence. With each breath, gently expand the space and imagine your body filling with soft light, illuminating any areas of your mind, body, or soul that hold pain or distress. Let the light softly warm your sadness about your loved one, opening and expanding the space within where you hold your grief.

And finally, let peace fill the space within . . . let the space deepen and expand as the peace fills more and more space. Peace and softness, however you imagine and feel them, are spreading throughout your body. And now expanding outside of yourself as though the energy of loving kindness and forgiveness that IS peace gently wraps itself around you . . . and you find yourself floating in the essence of peace, within you and all around you. In this moment, you are peace, and you have peace to share with your loved one. Breathe in the peace. Exhale the peace and surround your loved one with it. Moment by moment, breath by breath, you share the quality of peace. Breath by breath, moment by moment, you are peace.

A HEALING MEDITATION
FOR GRIEF

M editation can be useful for relaxing a grieving mind and an aching heart. Through meditation you can learn to focus your mind, let go of critical or negative inner voices, relieve your stress, and soften your grief. Meditation can relax the mind and body and teach you to accept whatever it is you are challenged by. Because heard meditations are usually more effective than read ones, either record it and play it back or have someone read it to you. It's a simple meditation you can memorize after a few practices and then do silently on your own.

> *Sit softly with your grief and close your eyes. Imagine your eyes being able to gently perceive everything inside your body. Let your eyes find your grief inside, any distress or sadness or physical pain. Find the place or places in your body where you are holding your grief. It may be locked in your throat so that you feel that it is difficult to swallow. Or you might feel a tight knot in your stomach, or a heaviness like lead through the core of your chest. Wherever you find your grief, let your awareness attend to it as though your heart were seeing the*

pain. Let your heart extend itself into the center of your grief, sending loving compassion. Allow love to flow into the pain of your grief. Allow your grief to receive the love and be softened by it.

Imagine the dense, heavy, hard qualities to your grief beginning to soften as you allow just a little flow of love to touch your pain. Now allow the love to continue to flow and imagine the hard fist around your grief begin to loosen its grip, open its hand, and make room for the grief to drift away. You do not need to force it or direct it out of your body; your natural instinct is toward healing.

Healing happens as the grief softens. Healing is happening now as you direct your attention, sending love . . . to that place that hurts. Let love touch your grief, that place that wants to be healed. Only pain is released, never the connection and love between you and your loved one. You allow the pain to be set free, so that there is more space within to feel and remember the love. Let go and release any fragments of holding, of pain, of grief. Let the space be filled with love and put the image of your loved one at the heart and center of that open space. Let yourself feel love, now that grief has made room for more.